THE UNIVERSAL MILLIONAIRE
— MINDFRAME —
PLAN, ACT, GROW, REPEAT

A SERIAL ENTREPRENEURS DREAM BOOK TO KICKSTART AND MAINTAIN A DREAM LIFE

Dr. T. Anderson Ph.D

THE UNIVERSAL MILLIONARE PLAN:
Act, Grow, Repeat

Copyright © 2020 *Dr. T. Anderson Ph.D*

All rights reserved.

All rights reserved. No portion of this book may be reproduced by any mechanical, photographic, or electronic process, or in the form of phonographic recording; nor may it be stored in a retrieval system, transmitted, or otherwise be copied for public or private use-except for brief quotations embodied in articles and reviews-without prior written permission of the publisher.

Printed in United States of America

CONTENTS

1 | WEALTH BUILDING AND LIFE CHOICES   1

2 | BUSINESS ENTERPRISE STRATEGIES   35

3 | BUDGETING AND WEALTH GROWTH   47

4 | BUILDING A SUCCESSFUL BUSINESS   77

5 | BUILDING BUSINESS CREDIT   137

6 | HOUSE PURCHASING   171

7 | REAL ESTATE WHOLESALING   189

8 | MAKING TRAVEL PLANS   237

1
WEALTH BUILDING AND LIFE CHOICES

Building wealth requires settling on a decision. One day you wake up, you take a gander at your life and ask, "What game am I playing?" How wealthy am I aspiring to be? How do I get there?

Notwithstanding the explanation, it's minutes like these that make a difference. They make a window of clearness to see your life from the outside. At these minutes, you can stop and ask yourself, "Is the manner in which I'm deciding to live my life driving me to the future that I truly need?" We all are, somewhat, sleepwalking through our lives. In any case, in these intelligent minutes, we have the chance to inquire as to whether our lives are following the lives we would pick if we could have anything we wanted.

THE RIGHT TO BE RICH

Whatever pose you may like to take in commendation of destitution, the reality remains that it is beyond the realm of imagination to expect to live a geniunely complete or, on the other hand, fruitful life except if one is rich. No individual can ascend to the most prominent conceivable peak of his ability or soul advancement except if he has much cash.

Individuals create at the top of the priority list, soul, and body by utilizing what they have around. Society is sorted-out to such an extent that individuals must have the cash to turn into the owner of those things. Accordingly, the premise of all human headway must be the study of getting wealthy. The object of all life is advancement. Everything that lives has a basic right to all the advancement it is fit for achieving. An individual's entitlement to life implies his entitlement to have the free and unhindered utilization of the considerable number of things which might be necessary to his fullest mental, profound, and physical unfurling at the end of the day, his entitlement to be rich.

In this book, we shall not examine wealth in an allegorical manner. To be extremely rich doesn't intend to be fulfilled or placated with a bit. No individual should be happy with a little, on the off chance that he is fit for utilizing and appreciating more. The motivation behind nature is the headway and improvement of life.

Each individual ought to have all that can add to the force, style, magnificence, and extravagance of life.

The individual who possesses all he needs for living the way he pleases and is well-equipped is wealthy. No one can have all he needs without much cash. Life has progressed up until this point and turns out to be mind-boggling to the fact that even the most customary man or lady requires an extraordinary measure of wealth to live in a way that, indeed, even methodologies culminate. Each individual typically needs to turn out to be all that he is fit for turning out to be; this craving to acknowledge intrinsic potential outcomes is inalienable in human instinct. Accomplishment in life is turning out to be what you need to be. You can become what you need to be as it were by utilizing things, and you can have the free utilization of things just as you become rich enough to purchase them. Accordingly, a comprehension of the study of getting rich is the most fundamental of all information.

The craving for wealth is the longing for a more extravagant, more full, and increasingly inexhaustible life. What's more, that longing is admirable. The individual who doesn't want to live all the more bounteously is phenomenal. What's more, the person who doesn't want to have cash enough to purchase all he needs may not be living to his maximum capacity. There are three thought processes in which we live: we live for the body, the psyche, and the spirit. None of these is preferred or holier over the other. Each is attractive; furthermore, neither one of the bodies, brains, or souls can live entirely on the off chance that one of the others is stopped of full life and articulation. It is not right or respectable to live just for the spirit and deny the brain or body. It isn't right to live for the astuteness and deny body and soul. We are altogether familiar with the odious outcomes of living for the body and rejecting both personalities, what's more, soul. We see that simple methods the total articulation of all that an individual can give forward through body, brain, and soul. No individual can be happy or, on the other hand, fulfilled except if his body is living entirely in each work and except if the equivalent is valid for his psyche and his spirit. Any place there is an unexpressed probability or, on the other hand, an unperformed capacity, there is an unsatisfied want. Want is probability looking for articulation or capacity looking for execution.

An individual can't live completely without excellent nourishment, open to apparel, a comfortable haven, and opportunity from exorbitant work. Rest and diversion are too crucial to his real life. He can't live completely at the top of the priority list without books and time to contemplate them without an open door for movement, perception, or scholarly friendship. To live completely at the top of the priority list, he should have scholarly entertainments and must encircle himself with all the objects of craftsmanship and excellence; he is fit for utilizing and increasing in value.

To live entirely in the soul, an individual must have love. Also, the declaration of affection is regularly baffled by neediness. A person's most noteworthy bliss is observed in the bestowal of advantages on those he adores. Love discovers its generally standard and unconstrained articulation in giving. The individual who has nothing to give can't fill his place as a spouse or father, resident, or individual. In the utilization of material things, an individual finds full life for his body, builds up his psyche, and unfurls his soul. It is in this way of incomparable significance to be rich. It is splendidly right that you should want to be rich. On the off chance that you are a typical man or lady, you can't help. It is consummately right that you ought to concentrate on the study of getting rich since it is the noblest and generally vital of all examines. On the off chance that you disregard this investigation, you are forsaken in your obligation to yourself, to God, and humankind. You can render God and humanity no more noteworthy help than to take advantage of yourself.

The thoughts of wealth in one's mind is the main force that can create unmistakable wealth from the unformed substance. The stuff from which everything is made is a substance which thinks. A thought of structure in this substance delivers the structure.

Each structure and procedure you find in nature is the precise articulation of an idea in the first substance. We live in an ideal world, and this world is a piece of a perfect universe. The view of a moving universe stretched out all through the indistinct substance. The reasoning stuff coming about from that idea appeared as frameworks of planets also, continue to keep up that form. The thinking substance appears as its idea and moves as per the concept. Holding the possibility of a hovering arrangement of suns and universes, it seemed as these bodies moved them in like manner.

Although the work might require hundreds of years, by speculating the type of a moderate developing tree, the unformed substance delivers the tree. In the making, the shapeless substance appears to move, as indicated by the lines of movement it has built up. The idea of an oak tree doesn't cause the momentary development of a fully developed tree. However, it starts moving the powers, which will create the tree along built-up lines of development.

Each idea of structure, held in deduction substance, causes the formation of that structure, however consistently, or at least for the most part, along the lines of development and activity as of now set up. On the off chance that the idea of a place, of a specific development, was put forth for the amorphous substance, it may not cause the moment arrangement of that house. In any case, it would cause the turning of creative energies as of now working in exchange and trade into such channels as to bring about the rapid structure of the house. What's more, if there were no current channels through which the inventive vitality could work, the house would be shaped straightforwardly from base substance- without hanging tight for the reasonable procedures of the natural and inorganic world. No idea of structure can be put forth for the unique substance without causing the formation of that structure.

Every form of wealth which an individual can achieve is a product of his or her thoughts. He can't shape a thing until he has believed that he can make it happen. What's more, so far, man has restricted his endeavors entirely to crafted by his hands; he has applied physical work to the universe of structures trying to change or modify previously existing structures. He has never thought of endeavoring to produce new structures by dazzling his contemplations upon the undefined substance.

First, we state that there is one unique, shapeless substance from which everything is made. All the numerous components are just various introductions of one element. All the numerous structures found in natural and inorganic nature are just different shapes produced using similar stuff. What's more, this stuff is thinking stuff; an idea held in it delivers the type of the idea. Thought, in speculation substance, produces shapes. A person is a reasoning focus, equipped for a unique concept. On the off chance that an individual can convey his idea to a unique reasoning substance, he can cause the creation or development of the thing he contemplates. To outline this:

There is a thinking stuff from which all things are made, and which, in its unique state, saturates, enters, and fills the interspaces of the universe. An individual can shape things in his idea, and by putting forth his idea for amorphous substance, can cause something he ponders to be made.

I can demonstrate these announcements using both rationale and experience. Thinking once more from the wonders of structure and thought, I come to one unique reasoning substance. Furthermore, thinking forward from this reasoning substance, I go to the person's capacity to cause the arrangement of the thing he ponders.

By test, I see this thinking as evident, and this is my most grounded confirmation. If one individual who peruses this book gets rich by doing what I guide him to do, that is proof on the side of my case. Besides, if each individual who does what I teach him to do gets rich, that is sure evidence until somebody experiences the process and falls flat. The hypothesis is valid until the procedure falls flat, and this procedure won't come up short because each individual who does precisely what I instruct him to do will get rich. I have said that an individual gets rich by doing things with a specific goal in mind. To do such, an individual must get ready to think with a particular goal in mind. An individual's method for doing things is the immediate consequence of the way he considers things.

Each individual has the standard and inalienable force to think what he needs to consider; however, it requires far more exertion to do than to think the contemplations proposed by appearances. To think, as indicated by appearances, is simple. To think truth paying little heed to appearances is difficult and requires more force than some other work an individual needs to perform.

There is no work from which many people recoil as they do from that of supported and back to back though; it is the most demanding work on the planet. This is particularly obvious when the truth is in opposition to appearances. Each appearance in the noticeable world will, in general, produce a relating structure in the mind that watches it. This must be forestalled by holding the idea of reality.

To view sickness's presence will deliver the type of malady as far as you could tell and at last in your body. Instead, you should hold the idea of reality, which is that there is no sickness. Illness is just an appearance and wellbeing. To view the appearances of neediness will create comparing structures as far as you could tell. You should hold to the reality that there is no destitution; there is just wealth. It expects capacity to think wellbeing when encompassed by the appearances of illness or to think wealth amidst the appearances of privation. Be that as it may, he who gets this force turns into brains. He can conquer destiny; he can have what he needs.

This influence must be obtained by getting hold of the virtual certainty behind all appearances: that there is one deduction substance, from which everything is made. At that point, we should get a handle on the reality that each idea held in this substance turns into a structure and that an individual can present his contemplations for it to cause them to take the frame and become unmistakable things.

When we understand this, we lose all uncertainty and dread since we realize that we can make what we need to make. We can get what we need to have and can become what we need to be. As an initial move toward getting rich, you should accept the three essential explanations given beforehand in this part. All together to underscore them, I will rehash them here:

There is a thinking stuff from which all things are made, and which, in its along the lines of the state, saturates, infiltrates, and fills the interspaces of the universe. An idea in this substance creates what is imaged by the idea. An individual can frame things in his idea, and by putting forth his idea for amorphous substance, can cause the thing he considers to be made.

You should drop every single other idea of the universe than this monistic one. You should abide upon this until it is fixed in your psyche and has gotten your constant idea. Peruse these doctrine articulations, what's more, over once more. Fix each word upon your memory; what's more, reflect upon them until you solidly accept what they state. On the off chance that uncertainty comes to you, give it aside a role as a transgression. Try not to tune in to contentions against this thought; don't go to places of worship or talks where an opposite idea of things is instructed or lectured. Try not to understand magazines or books which show an alternate thought. On the off chance that you get stirred up in your confidence, every one of your endeavors will be futile. Try not to inquire why these things are valid, nor theorize concerning how they can be valid. In essence, accept them based on previous experience — the study of getting rich starts with the full acknowledgment of this confidence.

HOW RICHES COME TO YOU

When I state that you don't need to drive sharp deals, I didn't imply that you don't need to drive any deals at all or that you are over the need for having any dealings with others. I imply that you shouldn't manage them unjustifiably; you do not need to get something to no end. You can give each person more than you take from him. You can't give an individual more in real money esteem than you take from him, yet you can give him more esteem than the money estimation of the thing you take from him. The paper, ink, and other material in this book may not merit the cash you paid for it. In any case, if the thoughts in this book bring you a large number of dollars, you have not been wronged by the individuals who offered it to you. They have given you excellent use of an incentive for a little money esteem.

Let's imagine that I possess an image that is worth a huge number of dollars in any cultivated network. I take it to the Baffin Bay, and by "persuasiveness" actuate an Eskimo to give a heap of hides worth $500 for it. I have genuinely wronged him since he has no utilization for the image. It has no utilization incentive to him; it won't add to his life. Yet, assume I give him a firearm worth $50 for his hides. At that point, he has made a decent deal. He has a use for the firearm; it will get him more hides and much nourishment; it will add to his life inside and out; it will make him rich. When you ascend from the serious to the inventive plane, you can check your business exchanges strictly. If you see that you are selling an individual anything which doesn't add more to his life than the thing he gives you in return, you can stand to stop it.

You do not have to defeat your competitors every time. However, if you are in a business that doesn't thrive well when it comes to beating opponents, you might reconsider opting for a different line. Give each more incentive than you take from him. At that point, you are adding to the life of the world with each business exchange. On the off chance that you have individuals working for you, you should take from them more in real money esteem than you pay them in compensation. In any case, you can arrange your business with the goal that it will be loaded up with the rule of headway. In this way, every representative who wishes to do so may propel a minimal consistently.

You can cause your business to accomplish for your representatives what this book is accomplishing for you. You can direct your business with the goal that it will be a stepping stool by

Dr. T. Anderson

which each willing representative may move to wealth himself. Also, it is not your issue if he doesn't acknowledge the chance.

Even though you can make your wealth out of the indistinct substance which permeates all of your condition, it doesn't follow that your fortune will quickly come to fruition from the air and appear before your eyes. On the off chance that you need a sewing machine, for example, I propose that before you dazzle the idea of a sewing machine on the reasoning substance, you first make sure the picture of the device is in your mind. On the off chance that you need a sewing machine, hold the psychological image of it with the best sureness that it is being made or is en route to you. After once shaping the idea, have the most outright and unquestioning confidence that the sewing machine is coming. Never think of it or discuss it without feeling confident that it will show up. Guarantee it as of now yours.

It will be brought to you by the intensity of the incomparable knowledge, following up on the psyches of men. On the off chance that you live in Maine, it might be that an individual will be brought from Texas or Japan to take part in a few exchanges, which will bring about your getting what you need. Assuming this is the case, the entire issue will be as a lot to that individual's favorable position for what it's worth to yours.

Remember for a minute that the reasoning substance is in all things, speaking with all the fixings, what's more, ready to impact everything. The longing of the thinking substance for more life and better living has caused the formation of all the sewing machines that have ever been made, and it can cause the creation of millions more. It will do so at whatever point individuals set it moving by want, confidence, and acting in a certain way.

You can have a sewing machine in your house. You can have anything you need, as long as you use it for the progression of your own life and the lives of others. You need not stop for a second about asking generally. "It is your Father's pleasure to give you the realm," said Jesus.

The first substance needs to live as much as conceivable in you; it requires you to have all that you can or, on the other hand, will use for the living of the most plentiful life. Your confidence gets invulnerable if you fix upon your awareness that the longing you feel for the ownership of wealth is unified with the longing of the Preeminent Power for progressively complete articulation.

When I saw a young man sitting at a piano and vainly attempting to bring concordance out of the keys, I saw that he was lamented and incited by his failure to play genuine music. I asked him for what reason he was despondent, and he replied, "I can feel the music in me, yet I can't cause my hands to go right." The music in him was the inclination of the divine Substance, containing all the potential outcomes of all life. All that there is of music was looking for articulation through the youngster.

God, the One Substance, is attempting to live and do and appreciate things through humanity. He is stating, "I need hands to assemble brilliant structures, to play divine harmonies, to paint wonderful pictures. I need feet to get my things done, eyes to see my delights, tongues to advise strong facts and to sing grand melodies."

Dr. T. Anderson

The craving you feel for wealth is the Infinite, looking to communicate in you as he tried to discover articulation in the young man at the piano. You need not stop for a second to ask to a great extent. Your part is to center and express the wants of God. There is the possibility that God has completed his work and has made all that he can make-that the majority of humanity must remain poor because it isn't sufficient to go around. Individuals hold to this mistaken idea to such an extent that they feel embarrassed to request wealth. They attempt not to need more than a discreet fitness just enough to make them genuinely agreeable.

I now review the instance of one understudy who was told that he should find in his mind a way to get the things he wanted with the goal that the innovative idea of them may be dazzled on the nebulous substance. He was a feeble man, living in a leased house and having just what he earned from the everyday. He proved unable to handle the way that all wealth was his. In this manner, after thoroughly considering the issue, he concluded that he might sensibly request another carpet for the floor of his best room and an anthracite coal stove to warm the house during the chilly climate. Adhering to the guidelines given in this book, he acquired these things in a couple of months. At that point, it unfolded upon him that he had not asked enough. He experienced the house where he lived and arranged every one of the enhancements he might want to make in it. He intellectually included a sound window here also, a room there. He proceeded until it finished in his brain as his optimal home. Furthermore, at that point, he arranged its goods.

Holding the entire picture in his psyche, he started living in a specific way and pushing toward what he needed. He claims the house now and is modifying it as per his psychological picture. Presently, with still more immense confidence, he is continuing to get more prominent things. It has been unto him as per his confidence, and it is so with you what's more, with us all.

The Programmed Life

A significant number of us lead a "customised life." Much of what we do is dictated by our culture, family, values, companions, instruction, profession, and money related status. For model, Paul's folks believed that training and filling in as an expert—an attorney, specialist, or designer—was the correct way for him. Consider it. Possibly your folks were hands-on, white-collar class, as Paul's, and put stock in the worth of proper instruction and an expert profession as a specialist or designer. Twenty a long time later, you've settled on life decisions that please your family and tail somebody else's thought of what's ideal for you, yet you abhor your profession. Recalling these decisions, does it, despite everything, serve you to live by another person's principles? Does it indeed, even truly help them?

Why Wealth Matters

It is essential to recognize what makes a difference to you in your life. Wealth doesn't generally matter, except if you don't have any. In any case, when you do have enough cash to meet your essential needs, the main thing is the thing that you can do with it. For instance, money permits you to offer your youngsters the chance to get excellent training. Cash enables you to get incredible human services. You can likewise travel all the more effectively and add to extraordinary causes when you have cash. Sounds like enjoyment, correct? But then money, despite everything, doesn't make a difference.

All in all, what makes a difference at that point? Everybody's answers will fluctuate, so we energize you to arrive at your own decisions as you consider this significant inquiry. Be that as it may, we're going to give you a clue: It's not cash. Numerous individuals liken wealth to material products and ventures, for example, vehicles, houses, what's more, taking luxurious get-aways. How often have you heard the expression, "Cash isn't all that matters"? We concur—to some degree. All in all, what is wealth at that point? What esteem does it have at its center?

At the point when you strip away the entirety of your material belongings, any assumptions of "easy street," and every one of your connections, you are left with three things:

1. Health.
2. Family/Relationships.
3. Freedom

Think for a minute: Can cash get you wellbeing? Indeed, it depends on who you ask and when you ask them. On the off chance that you ask previous wealthy person Steve Jobs, the appropriate response is "no." He passed on of malignant pancreatic growth at 56 years old. No measure of cash could have mended his malignancy ridden body. Be that as it may, if you consider the about 800 million individuals who don't approach clean water or adequate nourishment, only a tad of cash would "get" them a ton of wellbeing. Would money be able to get your time? If you ask a perishing man or lady, at most cash can get them just a limited quantity of time. Cash isn't acceptable at purchasing time that is as of now lost. Be that as it may, cash—whenever spent well—can get you future time. For model, Paul's nephew as of late rode a transport 26 hours from Chicago to Boston to see his cousin's graduation. In this case, $500 could have gotten him a plane ticket home and spared him 20 hours.

Would money be able to get your family and connections? Once more, it relies upon whom you inquire. If you have a stressed association with your family, odds are you're going to need to accomplish more than compose a check. You'll have to chip away at modifying those significant connections. Be that as it may, on the off chance that you are a barren couple hoping to receive a kid, cash can help you build a family. It's every one of them a matter of point of view. The more we considered it, the more we understood that cash is a type of vitality synonymous with the decision, or, even better, opportunity.

Wealth Brings Freedom

At the point when you express yes to wealth, you're stating yes to your potential for opportunity." Opportunity is the ability to pick and make. At the point when you express yes to wealth, you're saying yes to your potential for opportunity. You recognize the intensity of probability in your life.

The wealthy are allowed to convey what needs be as they seem to be—kind and giving or egotistical and unendurable. As Will Smith stated, "Cash and achievement don't change individuals; they just enhance what is as of now there." Without wealth, your decisions are restricted, and we accept this bargains your satisfaction, work, and wellbeing. Wealth makes opportunity, and opportunity is a definitive blessing throughout everyday life.

Building Wealth Is Saying "Yes" to Yourself

The exercises we share with you we learned through close to home understanding (both wins and misfortunes) and from cautiously watching others and their methodologies to building and keeping up wealth and sound and joyful lives. Wealth assembling influences your own and expert connections and moves your everyday viewpoint. As you decide to grasp wealth and experience more prominent decisions, after some time, you will feel a feeling of increased quiet, fulfillment, and real security—and not merely of the material assortment. Building wealth is a method for saying "yes!" to yourself and to those things that are imperative to you. It's a method to line up with all that you love and not rouse you on your excursion every day. By embracing a wealthy outlook and rehearsing the aptitudes we suggest in the sections ahead, you find a workable pace that makes the difference most. Wealth assembling influences your own also, professional connections, and rouses your everyday viewpoint.

Characterizing Entrepreneurs and Entrepreneurship

In this section, a lot of references will be made to the great consultant Peter Drucker. The business person has been characterized as one who begins his or her own, new, independent company. In any case, as Drucker called attention to, " Not each new independent company is pioneering or speaks to the business enterprise. " The couple who open a café in the Beijing rural areas without a doubt face a challenge. Be that as it may, would they say they are business visionaries? What they have done has been done commonly previously.

They bet on the expanding prominence of eating out in their zone; however, they have not made new buyer fulfillment or new buyer request. In this viewpoint, as indicated by Drucker, they are doubtlessly not business visionaries, even though theirs is another adventure. They may likewise have been purchasing work the same number of proprietors of extremely private companies do. The incomes and the net benefits of an exceptionally independent venture might be close to the person who could win as compensation for an organization. As a result, these agents have obtained their employments. Then again, Drucker referred to McDonald's, for instance, of business enterprise through the use of the executives' ideas and procedures, for example, institutionalizing the " item."

As per Drucker, business people and enterprises are particular highlights of an individual or an association. Additionally, the association shouldn't belittle, and new to be a business person since huge and frequently old ventures are polishing business as on account of 3M, which Drucker referred to as one of the most innovative organizations around, having created more than 60,000 new items. As per Drucker, business in this manner "Is a ' conduct ' as opposed to a character ' characteristic ' whose establishment lies in idea and hypothesis as opposed to instinct. Business people consider a change to be the standard and as solid. They usually don't bring about change themselves. Be that as it may, and this recognizes the business person from enterprise—the business visionary consistently looks for development, reacts to it, and endeavors it as a chance.

Development and Innovation

Development

Drucker had consistently focused on that the motivation behind a business is to make a client. In this way, in his view, the business venture had two—and just two—essential capacities: advertising and advancement. The second capacity of a business is development, the arrangement of distinctive financial fulfillment.

Drucker defined development, "As the errand of blessing human what's more, material assets with a new and more prominent wealth-creating limit. " He developed this: "Administrators must change over society's needs into open doors for a profitable business. That, as well, is the meaning of innovation." This is steady with the means referred to in the Vital Management Process as portrayed earlier and evaluating the association's outer condition to recognize open doors for development and development.

One model he referred to was the Penicillium form. It was an irritation, not an asset. Bacteriologists made a considerable effort to ensure their bacterial societies against pollution by shape until, in the 1920s, a London specialist understood that this vermin was accurately the bacterial executioner that had been looked for since quite a while ago. The shape became a significant asset. At long last, Drucker proposed, "Innovation isn't an invention. Innovation is a term of financial aspects instead of technology."

Types and Requirements of Innovation

Drucker stated: "It isn't sufficient for the business to give only any monetary merchandise and ventures; it must give better and then some monetary ones." He brought up, "The most profitable development is an alternate item or administration making another potential fulfilment, as opposed to improvement." An examination by the counseling firm Booz, Allen and Hamilton, during the 1980s, identified sorts of advancement as comprising of new product offerings, augmentations to current product offerings, enhancements or modifications of existing product offerings (which is the place most inventive action happens as indicated by the study), repositioning of items, cost decreases, and new-to the - world items, which was distinguished as comprising of not precisely 10 percent everything being equal. A lot of Drucker's emphasis was on new - to - the - world items, although he mentioned a few other creative chances.

Dr. T. Anderson

Sudden Successes and Unexpected Failures

Drucker proposed the best potential hotspot for fruitful development is from an Unexpected Success or Failure. Abuse of this requires investigation basically because a sudden achievement is a manifestation. Assume that one specific item in the business' product offering beats every other item past the administration's desires. For what reason is that happening? A contender is having unforeseen achievements in a specific market section. The executives must find out why this is going on, asking themselves what it would mean on the off chance that they abused it. A great model goes back to the good old days when Marriott was a café network before it ventured into inns. The board saw that one of its cafés in Washington, DC, was outflanking all others in the chain as far as the month to month incomes. Upon examination, the eatery was situated opposite Hoover Field, the city's first air terminal. Before carriers served dinners on planes, Marriott found that carrier travelers would stop by the eatery and buy sandwiches and bites to take on the plane with them. Marriott met with the old Eastern Airlines and proposed to nourish to be served on the aircraft—in this manner; it started the aircraft cooking business.

Surprising Failures can likewise prompt different open doors for development as proposed by the accompanying citation by a previous Chief of Johnson and Johnson, and another firm Drucker distinguished as being inventive.

In another model, the Ford Motor Company built up a new vehicle, the Edsel, in 1957. As far as anyone knows, the auto's plan originated from broad statistical surveying about client inclinations in appearance and styling. Yet, the Edsel turned into a complete disappointment following it was presented—perhaps the biggest disappointment in the historical backdrop of the car business.

Rather than accusing the "unreasonable shopper," Ford's administration concluded something was happening that was not in line with general car industry suppositions about shopper conduct. In the wake of reinvestigating the market, the organization found another "way of life fragment" to which it immediately reacted by creating the wonderfully structured and delivered Thunderbird model — perhaps the best achievement in US auto history. Passage ought to maybe return to this experience today, alongside the other two US automakers, as they endeavor to endure Japanese automobile producers' developing test.

You can gain from progress; however, you need to work at it; it's much simpler to gain from disappointment. Lewis Lehr, previous CEO, 3M Corporation An exemplary model is 3M's Post-It takes note of, the little yellow stick-on used in workplaces all through the world. They were initially to be utilised in a modern application, however, fizzled. Afterward, a 3M researcher who took an amount of the material home found his little girl had cut up a portion of these sheets and utilized them to post notes on the fridge, helping her mom remember what to purchase at the grocery store. From this disappointment, advanced an item that 3M has been selling for a considerable time. Has your business had any victories or disappointments that maybe ought to be researched further?

Dr. T. Anderson

Ambiguities

Drucker portrayed an ambiguity as a disparity, a discord, between what is and what " should " to be, or between what is and what everyone expects it to be. Like the unforeseen occasion, regardless of whether achievement or disappointment, a disjointedness indicates the change that has just happened or change that can be made to occur. As per Drucker, there are a few sorts of confusion: A confusion between an industry's financial substances. Incoherency inside the cadence or rationale of a procedure Incoherency Between the Economic Realities of an Industry Drucker called attention to that if interest for an item or administration is developing consistently, its monetary exhibition ought to relentlessly improve, as well. It should effortlessly be profitable in an industry with the relentlessly rising request since the tide conveys it. An absence of productivity in such an industry recommends a confusion between monetary substances.

This kind of ambiguity commonly happens inside an entire industry or then again an entire-assistance segment and shows a significant opportunity of development for an exceptionally centered new endeavor, new procedure, or on the other hand, further assistance. Likewise, the pioneer who abuses this incoherency can rely on hardly any contenders for quite a while before they wake up to the truth that they have a new and dangerous challenge. The beginning of the "smaller than usual" steel plant effectively abusing incoherency before administering the more significant coordinated steel processes in the United States acknowledged what was happening in the business. What disjointed qualities can be abused in the different companies that you have watched?

Disjointedness Between the Reality of an Industry and the Assumptions About It

This kind of incoherency happens when the industry board has confusion about its industry's actual situation and hence makes wrong presumptions about it, coming about in misled endeavors. Drucker focuses on the zone where results don't exist and offer an open door for a trendsetter who can see and adventure it. Drucker referred to a case of this ambiguity in the maritime vessel industry that was accepted to be biting the dust during the 1950s. The significant supposition about the business was that the ship's principal cost was while it was venturing out from direct A toward point B.

Significant endeavors were aimed at getting quicker and progressively productive boats, fewer group individuals, etc., to lessen costs. A trailblazer presumed that these suspicions about the industry weren't right. The significant expenses were while the ship was inactive in port, hanging tight for freight emptying and new payload to be stacked. The outcome was the advancement of the payload compartment, the rollon, move off the ship, and the holder's vessel. By and large, expenses were diminished by 60 percent, and the business has developed significantly from that point forward. The transportation compartment was created by Malcolm McLean in the late 1950s and saw its unique application by the legislature in delivery supplies for the Vietnam War.

Disjointedness Between the Efforts of an Industry and the Values and Desires for its Customers everything being equal, this one might be the most well-known. Makers and providers normally confound what it is the client purchases. They accept that what is " esteem " to them is similarly of " esteem " to the client, whose desires and qualities are typically extraordinary. The client sometimes sees what the person in question is purchasing as what the maker or provider conveys.

While makers and providers may whine about " silly " client conduct, there are potential open doors for an exceptionally explicit and centered advancement. Various models exist of individuals exploiting this ambiguity, with a fruitful development, for example, by the Edward Jones Company, a money related assistance firm, abusing the misperceptions of more prominent Wall Road firms comparative with client esteems. Jones recognized a market portion, ranchers and individuals going to resign, as having a craving for protected speculation before their retirement rather than the visiting merchant of stocks that Wall Street firms concentrated on. As a result, it has gotten one of the most significant money-related administration firms in the United States.

Confusion Within the Rhythm or Logic of a Process

This confusion searches for something absent in a specific procedure, explicitly how a purchaser may utilize an item. The advancement of the Scotts Spreader to permit property holders to spread compost equitably is a case of exploiting this incoherency.

Procedure Needs

Advancements in Process Needs search for a frail or missing connection in a current procedure. Open doors for advancement exist if there is a perceived need to finish the procedure. It must be felt that there is a "superior way" to accomplish something eagerly gotten by clients. Here Drucker brought up that advancement here begins with the activity to be done and consummates a procedure that now exists.

As per Drucker, practical advancements dependent on process needs require five fundamental criteria. Drucker included that the requirement for a special way should be comprehended. A great case of this wellspring of development is the little known creator who made his name a piece of our jargon, Elijah McCoy. In 1870 he earned a qualification in building, yet as a dark man during the 1870s, the main occupation he could discover was an oiler on the Michigan Central Railroad. Trains needed to stop much of the time at that point and must be oiled by hand. McCoy figured out there must be a superior way and structured a greasing up cup that trickled oil onto the moving parts. His advancement turned into a hit; what's more, soon, no bit of powerful hardware was viewed as complete except if it had a McCoy lubricator. What's more, individuals taking a gander at a machine's lubricator start to pose an inquiry we're despite everything asking . . . is it the genuine article?

Dr. T. Anderson

Changes in Industry and Market Structures

Changes in industry and market structure, for the most part, occur because of evolving client inclinations, tastes, and qualities. Additionally, the fast development of a specific industry is a reliable marker of changing industry structures. Japanese entrance of the US auto advertise with littler and more eco-friendly vehicles during the 1970s permitted them to exploit changing buyer inclinations for automobiles, inspired to a great extent by sensational increments in gas costs (the cost of utilized Japanese fuel - productive cars, for example, Hondas and Toyotas had expanded impressively in mid-2008 because of gas selling for over $ 4 per gallon). Drucker arranged the second arrangement of hotspots for the creative, open door, including changes outside the business or industry.

Changes in Demographics

Drucker felt that adjustments in socioeconomics (age, instruction, discretionary cash flow, a geographic move, etc.) are among the most concrete indicators of things to come and offer open doors for advancement. Those working together in China should investigate what openings a maturing populace, the one - kid family, or expanded extra cash in China offer for development.

Criteria for Process Need Innovations

1. An independent procedure.
2. One weak or missing link.
3. A succinct definition of the goal.

4. Specifications for the solutions which can be unmistakably characterized.
5. Widespread acknowledgment that "there should be a superior way."

Changes in Meaning and Perception

The prior discourse of Unforeseen Successes and Unexpected Failures exhibited that they are frequently a sign of an adjustment in observation and significance. The accomplishment of Ford's Thunderbird and the disappointment of its Edsel were ascribed to changes in observation. The car showcase that had consistently been divided by salary bunch was seen by clients as divided byways of life. Distinguishing open doors for advancement in this classification requires timing and judgment; are there genuine changes occurring in discernment, or just prevailing fashions that will be short-lived?

New Knowledge (Scientific and Nonscientific)

New information can be a wellspring of imaginative chances; however, as indicated by Drucker, it has the longest lead time of all wellsprings of advancements. There is a long time length between the rise of new information and when it gets relevant to innovation—in addition to the additional time before the design transforms into items in the commercial center. Another normal for knowledge based developments is that they are nearly never dependent on one factor yet on the assembly of various types of information. An exemplary case of the period from data to a business application is the fly motor, which was initially protected in 1930. Its first military test was in 1941, and the first business stream plane was the Comet in 1952. In the long run, Boeing built up the 707, and by 1958, it got operational, 28 years after the patent. Improvement of the new plane required combining the advancements of optimal design, new materials, and powers.

Finally, it is significant that information based advancement be clear in building up a vital (authority) position before others and that it has a reasonable spotlight available—to put it plainly, making a market for its items. Drucker referred to DuPont that didn't sell Nylon following creating it. The firm initially made a buyer showcase for ladies' hosiery and clothing produced using Nylon and a business opportunity for vehicle tires, likewise utilizing Nylon. At the point, DuPont offered the Nylon to makers to make the articles for which it had just made an interest.

Drucker also remarked on the Bright Idea as one of the significant wellsprings of licenses, yet barely any arrival at item improvement; furthermore, its prologue to the commercial center. He reasoned that Bright Thoughts are the most unsafe and most disastrous wellspring of imaginative openings.

The Principles of Innovation

Drucker detailed his Principles of Innovation:

1. Investigate the wellsprings of innovation for the emergence of new opportunities.
2. Decide client needs, wants, and desires.
3. Advancement ought to be basic and focussed.
4. Begin with small creation, then gradually work your way up

5. Development should focus on leadership.

Drucker indicates that straightforward and centered developments ought to be coordinated toward a specific, precise, and structured application, and should be centered around a particular need that it fulfills and the specific final product it produces. This is a practical necessity. On the off chance that the purchaser doesn't comprehend what the item does, the creative item won't sell. Notwithstanding the standards, he also referred to various things that should not be done comparative with development.

1. Do make an effort not to be shrewd: Drucker recommended that advancement not be excessively complex as "ineptitude, all things considered, is the main thing in a copious and never - bombing supply. "
2. Do not expand or chip endeavors: Essentially, center around the creative exertion and don't pursue such a large number of changes simulataneously.
3. Do not develop for the future: The advancement ought to have prompt application. Be that as it may, he included, " Innovative openings in some cases have extended lead times. In pharmaceutical research, ten years of innovative work are in no way, shape, or form unprecedented or especially long.
4. But then no pharmaceutical organization would fantasize about beginning an examination venture for something that doesn't, if practical, have quick application as a medication for medicinal services needs that now exist.

While not these thoughts left Drucker holes, it is useful to develop these focuses by offering a theoretical from the perspectives on Philip Kotler.

Qualities of Innovation Adoption

A few items get on quickly, while others take a long time to pick up acknowledgment. Five qualities impact the pace of reception of a development.

- The main is a relatively favorable position—how much the advancement seems better than existing items.
- The second is similarity—how much the advancement matches the qualities and encounters of the people.
- The third is unpredictability — how much the development is generally hard to comprehend or utilize.
- The fourth is distinguishableness — how much the development can be taken a stab at a constrained premise.
- The fifth is coherence — how much the gainful aftereffects of utilization are perceptible or describable to other people.

Different attributes that impact the pace of selection are cost, hazard and vulnerability, logical believability, and social endorsement. The new-item advertiser needs to investigate these elements and give the key one's most signfiicant consideration in planning the new item, furthermore, its advertising program. Drucker views that development should begin little, by and by 3M most likely outlines this rule best with its saying, "Make a bit, sell a little."

Drucker developed his rule that advancement should point at administration: "If a development doesn't focus on the initiative from the start, it is probably not going to be inventive enough, and along these lines probably not going to be fit for setting up itself." At that point, he explained this by showing that initiative could be in a specific market or a showcase specialty, which is more reasonable than endeavoring to win the world with another item.

2

Business Enterprise Strategies

Market Leadership and Dominance Objective

One fundmaental way for an entrepreneur to achieve a millionaire growth plan is to become a leader in whatever market he finds himself in. Being a leader in a market means you determine the pace of the industry's growth. You continuosly revolutionize the way things are done by developing new strategies and innovations for business advancement.

First, with the Most: This procedure hopes to achieve showcase authority, if not through and through predominance. To accomplish this, the new item (advancement) being presented must be more than an improvement. It must have significant item separation and be both new to the market and new to the client. Instances of organizations who have effectively executed this system and rapidly picked up showcase administration were Wang Laboratories and the presentation of the primary word processor, and Apple Computer with the presentation of the principal PC. Sony is maybe one of the better instances of utilizing this system considering the advancements it presented that made it the market head, for example, the first attractive recording device in 1950, the primary all-transistor radio in 1955, the principal pocket-sized radio in 1964, and the Sony Walkman in 1979.

Hit Them Where They are Not (Creative Imitation): This methodology points at market or industry authority; however, without the danger of making the advertising. It is intended to outflank the pioneer by imaginative impersonation by enhancing something that another person created. For this technique to work, the first item should be a triumph. Instances of fruitful execution of this system were IBM, presenting its PC after Apple made the market. The Japanese organization Seiko acquainting advanced watches with supplanting the more conventional Swiss watch developments. The two organizations, through inventive impersonation, immediately picked up advertise leadership.

Innovative Judo: Judo is the battling system that uses the other individual's quality and weight against him with the different moves to toss him down. Enterprising Judo searches for what the current market pioneers believe their qualities to be. It, at that point, bases its innovative technique on this. Usually, these pioneers have an obsession with the high-finish of the market and the most gainful one. They endeavor to offer everything in a solitary bundle, and they accept that quality is characterized by them as opposed to by the client—genuine instances of Drucker's Business Sins. Pioneering Judo accepts that the pioneers will proceed with their conduct as they sink into designs of unsurprising conduct and decline to change regardless of whether they are crushed. Standard, the Japanese copier maker, utilizing Entrepreneurial Judo and evaluating the conduct of Xerox, which was then the pioneer, had the option to effectively take a vast offer of the copier showcase away from Xerox, beginning with the low finish of the market and afterward in the end additionally taking an enormous portion of the high end. Another case of this system was MCI and Sprint utilizing AT&T's evaluating framework to remove a huge level of the long separation phone showcase in the United States.

Market Control and Monopoly Objective (High - Profit Specialty Strategies)

The goal of these systems is to acquire showcase control and become a restraining infrastructure in a specific, exceptionally beneficial market specialty. The objective is to be careful that, despite making the item or administration imperative, nobody is probably going to move into the specialty and attempt to contend.

Cost - Gate Strategy: This system involves building up an item or administration that is an imperative piece of a more effective procedure. The procedure works where some current advance in a procedure is off the mark with the various advancements and requires numerous activities, making the expense of utilizing the item in the long run superfluous. The development of the victory preventer for seaward oil wells is an exemplary case of this procedure. The expense of the preventer is insignificant versus the expense of tidying up a massive oil slick in the sea, a gigantic concern as progressively seaward penetrating is being prescribed to manage rising oil costs. Another necessity of this methodology is the market must be constrained to the point that whoever involves the specialty initially can bar any other individual from entering it. Then again, the danger of this system is that it offers constrained development potential since future development is subject to the extension of the general procedure. On the off chance that oil organizations are not boring seaward oil wells, the development potential for the offer of blow-out preventers is limited.

Claim to fame Skill Strategy: This technique includes evaluating openings in another or up and coming business sector or industry pattern and creating a high-expertise item or administration to serve the market. When the market starts to develop, the trendsetter has a critical head begin once again potential contenders and has just become a standard industry provider. An exemplary case of this technique is organisations that make brake cushions, electrical circuits, or headlamps that go into the production and gathering of vehicles. These organizations have been significant providers to the vehicle business for quite a long time, getting in right on time with the Specialty Skills Strategy. Hardly any individuals even know who these organizations are. Indeed, this tecnique's potential danger is that one must depend on another person to make a business opportunity for the business's establishment product.

Strength Market Niche Strategy: As indicated by Drucker, this is generally gainful of the Market Niche systems. The objective is to build up a claim to fame showcase specialty sufficiently large to be gainful, yet little enough not to make it advantageous for potential contenders to attack. A case of this technique was developing the American Express Travelers Checks for agents and vacationers, taking out the danger of conveying money on their movements. American Express overwhelmed this market spoecialty for a considerable length of time until banks included these administrations for their clients, with no administration charges. A more late-model was the Big Bertha golf driver created by Callaway Golf focused on the novice, end of the week golf player that was amazingly fruitful for a considerable length of time until others, for example, Taylor Made, entered the advertise with its driver. Savants' Views and Closing Drucker Gaps In our exchange of potential Drucker holes comparative with development; we asked whether Creative Imitation, Entrepreneurial Judo, Market Specialty, etc. are genuine " methodologies " or whether they are questions to ask during item advancement as to situating of the item— an advertising choice. For example, when an imaginative chance has been recognized (Drucker's Sources of Innovation), what kind of item should be created, and where should it be situated in the commercial center? The " how " it gets brought into the commercial center is the " methodology " that incorporates valuing, marking, channel, and different choices not referenced by Drucker.

Dr. T. Anderson

Other Contributors

While Drucker examined different procedures to present an advancement, his techniques didn't manage the numerous issues that should be thought about when propelling another item that regularly falls under the Four Ps of showcasing. Choices comparative with marking, valuing, choosing the suitable channels, etc., are missing from Drucker's exchange. However, he focused on the significance of showcasing as one of the " just " two elements of an association alongside advancement. In this manner, it was essential to incorporate a more far-reaching discourse of showcasing and its related instruments in our programs. Here we depended on the commitments of Philip Kotler and Roger Best to enhance Drucker's perspectives on the advertising component, as implied earlier.

I also included some different components of advancement that Drucker didn't cover, such as an exchange of the pace of appropriation of development, the developing idea of Disruptive Technologies by Clayton Christensen, as different wellsprings of development.

Why Disruptive Technologies Are Ignored Christensen extends on the last motivation behind why Disruptive Technologies (items) are disregarded and ascribed it to the current plan of action and procedures of organizations. Organizations center around advertise size and client needs and, along these lines, put resources into the advancement of higher worth-added items to sell at higher net revenues. This prompts the move in the weighted normal of item deals into continuously higher market levels—higher gross edges in higher market levels versus lower showcase levels. This model impacts what advancement recommendations will be embraced and given assets and which ones will be disregarded.

As Drucker had focused on, the intuition of good administration is to tune in to and react to client needs. Accordingly, significant clients are gotten some information about new thoughts and are solicited to survey the incentive from inventive items (center gatherings).

Development and Entrepreneurship

Since the ogranization's clients also endeavor to remain in front of their rivals regarding improving their items' presentation, they keep on requesting the best from their providers. Christensen reasons that lead clients are dependably exact in evaluating the potential for Sustaining Technologies yet are dependably off base for surveying the potential for Disruptive Technologies. In his view, " They are inappropriate people to inquire.

Defining Entrepreneurship Goals

Why Are Goals Important?

Similarly, as your last goal is imperative to your excursion, your objectives are imperative to your business. They characterize your goal and shape what your business will turn into. They additionally assist you in deciding a course of events for the things you need to do. Start by determining the reason(s) you need to begin a business. Would you like to rake in boatloads of cash? Would you like to be your possess chief? Would you like to give work to yourself or your family? Some potential explanations behind beginning a business are because you need to:

1. Have more power over your life and profession,
2. Increase your salary,
3. Make a distinction and add to society,
4. Reach your maximum capacity by accomplishing something you appreciate,
5. Use your accessible assets (work, land, accounts) all the more proficiently, or potentially
6. Diversify your benefits.

Consider your life as an entrepreneur and director, considering all parts of your life. The reasons individuals start a business fall inside four general business objectives: administration, social, benefit, or development. Administration, benefit, and development objectives are interrelated because most independent companies must give quality help if they need to make a benefit and develop. Numerous organizations have begun from a social motivation, for example, providing items that don't hurt the earth, have still had the option to accomplish the benefit objective. You should likewise consider how enormous you need the business to turn into. This is significant because one reason organizations fizzle is uncontrolled development. Think about whether you need the business to stay little or develop enough to challenge a bigger contender. Is your objective to get a benefit proportionate with your exertion and venture, or is it to get however much benefit as could reasonably be expected?

Defining Goals and Objectives

While objectives can be expansive or general, destinations ought to be clear and compact. Objectives don't need to be explicit enough to follow up on, yet they should give you a future objective or a rundown of things you need to deal with. Goals, be that as it may, should be SMART—Specific, Measurable, Action-oriented, Realistic, and Timely—to achieve the objectives set for your business.

Explicit goals ought to be as nitty gritty as could reasonably be expected. Altogether, for the goals to be quantifiable, you should state them as far as dollars or amounts. Goals are a way of execution you can use to assess the activity. Action-oriented targets state which moves should be made and who will take them. Targets ought to be practical yet testing, with set cutoff times to be opportune. Do you make goals toward the start consistently? Goals can be incredible assets. They can assist you in taking your business to the following level. The catch is, when you make a goal, you need to work to make it come genuine.

If you need an activity, you need an activity plan. Objective setting is the ideal way I know to change grand goals into main concern results. Research shows that when business visionaries set quantifiable objectives for themselves, they're increasingly similar to accomplish them. When you participate in an evident objective setting, you characterize your goals in practical, measurable terms. You likewise need to recognize the assets, time, and assets you'll require to contribute to achieving them. That is how you create activity plans. When you know where you need to go, the subsequent stage is to make sense of how you'll arrive and the amount you're ready to spend on the outing.

Utilize the SMART System

egarding the objective setting, the SMART framework is straightforward, rational, and gets the activity done. Every objective must be characterized, so it meets the accompanying criteria:

Specific, Achievable, and Realistic - Make sure your objectives are concrete, concise, and achievable. Rather than "I need to get significantly more cash-flow this year," determine "I need to increment my incomes by X per cent (a reasonable sum) before the year's over." Measurable - Frame your objectives in such a manner so you can quantify your advancement. For model, plan on estimating month to month or quarterly incomes against a year ago's figures- - something you ought to do in any case.

Timely - Give yourself a reasonable period for accomplishing your objective. At that point, break it down into littler, momentary augmentations. Everything being equal, you may not achieve that X percent expansion from the get-go in the year; however, you can progress in its direction. Partition your objective percent increment into a month to month or quarterly augmentations that permits you to expand on your energy.

This produces quantifiable, feasible, and transient objectives to seek after. Record your goals and activity anticipates paper. Regardless of whether you record them or type them, the very demonstration of recording them will help you éesh out your thoughts. Once your plans are finished, you'll have a nitty-gritty guide with headings to follow.

Survey your objectives and plans routinely. Make a month to month meeting with yourself if that is the stuff. This will help keep you on track as time unfurls. Additionally, be careful with "BHAGs"- - large, furry, brassy objectives. Super-aspiring objectives are incredible regarding long-ago arranging and basic leadership, yet they don't loan themselves to objective setting. Concentrate on achievable objectives that you can reasonably reach inside the year. It's anything but difficult to make goals, yet it's challenging to make them work out as expected. No big surprise, a few business visionaries create similar goals consistently while never accomplishing them. Try not to let yourself fall into that gathering. This year, make plans to set SMART objectives and activity plans.

Activity Plans

When you have recognized your destinations, the subsequent stage is to separate every target vigorously plans, or every one of the means essential to accomplish that target. Consider activity designs as little, sensible activities. Ensure the activity plans are short enough to be cultivated in a couple of days or seven days, all things considered. Work on the most auspicious objectives and goals, to begin with, separating them into the month to month activity plans.

Separating every target energetically plans will support you make the overwhelming undertaking of beginning another business sensible and less unpleasant. Starting a business takes thought and arranging. Understanding the reasons, you need to begin a business and set individual and business objectives, which are fundamental to your prosperity. Separating this procedure into three stages will make it less overwhelming and progressively sensible. In stage one, you should set wide objectives to be cultivated. For instance, you need to begin a business and get a 10% return on your venture, maybe your objective. In stage two, you should separate your objectives into objects that are SMART—explicit, quantifiable, activity situated, sensible, and auspicious. In stage three, you should additionally separate your targets into activity plans—littler, progressively practical tasks. This procedure won't just help you choose where you are going and how you will arrive, yet it will give a guide to your excursion.

3
BUDGETING AND WEALTH GROWTH

Setting up a financial limit is the demonstration of choosing the amount of your cash you will spend on one thing, how much on another, etc., before you're quite the situation of going through the money. Adhering to a spending limit is the demonstration of finishing on those choices. Making a spending limit isn't simple, yet adhering to any financial limit is very troublesome. Try to concentrate on the word sensible. It doesn't take a lot to look into or numerous problematic choices to conclude that you will spend $200 every month on nourishment. Be that as it may, on the off chance that you've never spent under $500 per month on nourishment, you'll destroy your spending right the first week.

Instead, before you start choosing the numbers in your financial limit, you'll have to thoroughly survey your present circumstance, truly investigate where you can reduce your budgetary commitments (both huge and little), rebuild your obligation (if fundamental) see whether you can include pay. **At precisely that point, are you prepared to choose reasonably where each penny will be spent.**

A financial limit is an instrument, and like all apparatuses, the outcomes you get from it will be controlled by how you use it. On the off chance that you make a sensible spending plan and stick to it, you can watch your life push ahead. If you set ridiculous budgetary desires and don't try to finish them, don't think your money related issues are completed.

Defining Budgetary Goals

When utilized effectively, a spending limit doesn't confine you; it engages you. You're going to set up a spending limit since you have monetary objectives that are not being met. For instance, you may need to:

- Have the option to cover every one of your tabs from your check—and possibly have a minimal left finished
- Purchase your first house Save for retirement; however, can't locate any additional cash to get begun
- Pay off the entirety of your Mastercards and never stray into the red again
- Give more money to your congregation or different philanthropies

- Work for yourself
- Getaway
- Prevent got notification from the emergency clinic about your hospital expenses
- Purchase another—or if nothing else more up to date—vehicle
- Remain at home with your infant
- Rebuild some portion of your home
- Pay for laser eye medical procedure
- Account, at any rate, some part of your youngster's advanced degree
- Purchase medical coverage
- Revamp your credit
- Figure out how to think about your maturing guardians
- At long last, form your fantasy house
- Withdraw from nonappearance from your business to work in the Peace Corps
- Return to class and start another profession
- Purchase the midtown coffeehouse when the present proprietors resign
- Get an entirely different closet

Are any of these your objectives?

Provided that this is true, planning will get you there, regardless of whether the changes appear to be outlandish at this moment. Regardless of whether you're stuck in a vocation, you try not to like, frantically need to return to class, need to deal with a maturing guardian, and have $19,000 in Visa obligation, you can meet your money related objectives—similarly to others have done before you. With a decent spending limit, a little tolerance, and a ton of assurance, you'll arrive in the long run.

Budgeting Tools

You may be enticed to address this inquiry with something astute like "cash." But on the off chance that you do that, you're overlooking the main issue. Making a financial limit isn't tied in with having cash; it's tied in with making sense of what you have, what you're spending it on, and how you can understand your fantasies. To do this, you'll need some essential devices.

A Computer

Individuals made spending plans in the previous days' PCs, and you can, in any case, make an impeccably decent one, sitting at the kitchen table with a pencil, a stack of paper, and a mini-computer. In any case, why not do things the simple way? On the off chance that you have a decent, working PC, set it to work for you. Make an envelope checked "Spending plan" (or something comparative) so you know where every one of your documents will go. If you have considerations about your spending limit and about ways you can set aside cash or additional wellsprings of pay you overlooked, note them down and hurl them into the "Financial limit" organizer. That way, they'll all be brought together, and you can get at them effectively.

The Right Software

There is a wide range of budgetary programming programs out there, each one claiming that it's just a single you need. I won't prescribe any of them specifically, even though on the off chance that you choose to utilize one, get a reasonable thought before you get it of what it's the contribution. You're introducing a period of mindful spending, so you would prefer not to buy something that isn't actually what you need or want. You can then sidestep each of those splendid, sparkling projects; what's more, take the necessary steps, and develop the spreadsheets yourself. It's most certainly not hard—as you'll find in the accompanying pages—and on the off chance that you have a quality spreadsheet program, for example, Microsoft Excel, you'll be fit as a fiddle.

Spending and Income Records

One objective you will achieve as you experience this book is keeping precise and cautious records of your costs and salary. In any case, it's conceivable that you've not been doing that up to now. Gather every one of your bills in a single spot, conceivably in an envelope or other compartments, so that you won't lose any of them. At your neighborhood office supply store, you can discover growing accordion organizers, each space set apart with the name of the month. In a different envelope or box, keep your compensation stub records. This applies regardless of whether you're paid with physical checks or through the direct store into your financial balance. You have to see precisely what's coming in and when you're accepting it. Keep the stubs in the request where you get them. Additionally, in this envelope, keep stubs of some other checks you get (charge returns, endowments, and so forth.) These records are fundamental both for planning and for charge purposes.

Most money related counsels prescribe keeping your monetary records for at any rate three years. This shouldn't be a tremendous weight; make sure you keep them arranged and someplace you can have simple access to them on the off chance that you need them. When it comes time to dispose of them, I unequivocally prescribe acquiring a reasonable shredder from an office supply store and destroying them. Along these lines, you limit the probability of data fraud.

Defining Budgetary Goals

Planning is tied in with getting from where you are money-wise to where you need to be. Furthermore, to do that, you must choose precisely where you'd prefer to wind up. Individuals regularly experience difficulty planning because they haven't generally plunked down and thought everything being equal about the sort of life they need and how they may pay for it. You will do things another way. You're going to begin by posing yourself some hard inquiries.

What Do You Want?

Meet Eva Sanders, age thirty-eight, whose spending we're going to look at to perceive how this procedure functions. Eva has worked at a similar organization for a long time, working up to the administration level a year ago. She purchased an apartment suite six years back, has a vehicle installment on a three-year-old vehicle, owes about $2,800 in charge card obligation, has some cash in reserve funds, is a single parent with two children (ages ten and fourteen), and takes an interest in the organization's 401(k) retirement plan. For the most part, Eva has enough cash to take care of the tabs at regular intervals, although the children's developing costs are beginning to pressure the family's pay.

Eva's concluded that she needs a sensible, feasible spending plan with a few objectives. Keeping that in mind, she's thought of the accompanying rundown:

- Help the children pay for school
- Pay off the Mastercard
- Resign
- Set aside some salary in an investment account

Notice that these are mostly entirely broad. That is fine at this stage. You can stand to be general; you're merely attempting to get a thought of what you'd like your life to resemble. Billie needs a real existence wherein her children are in school (or have graduated). To a great extent, she's obligation free, and she can retire with some cash to enhance her Social Security installments.

What's Realistic

Having defined a set of general objectives for herself, Eva needs to take a gander at them once more, this time to what's practical and sensible. We'd all like to resign promptly and live in a seashore house in Tahiti; however, that will not occur. Being realistic about her objectives doesn't mean Eva needs to abandon them; she needs to include a period and a few numbers. This is the thing that she thinks of:

Help the children pay for school. Pay for a large portion of the costs at one of the three colossal state colleges (right now $14,500 every year for educational cost, charges, room, and board) or put that equivalent sum toward a private or out-of-state school.

Pay off the charge card in nine months. Get the equalization to zero, and afterward, if it's utilized by any stretch of the imagination, take care of it in full each month.

Resign from the organization at age fifty (in twelve years). However, Eva's current pay is $49,248 after assessments before findings for protection and 401(k) commitments. Spare a half year of salary throughout the following twelve years. This cash would be for crises just, not to be contacted for any different costs.

We should experience these balanced objectives in more fine-grained detail.

Help the Kids Pay for College

It is incredible to pay the children's whole instruction costs, so they didn't need to assume understudy obligation. Be that as it may, Billie realizes she can't bear the cost of that. Instead, she makes two elective plans: one including in-state educational cost (on which she'll get a markdown); the other for an increasingly costly elective yet one that will mean the understudies were assuming more obligation.

When we come to consider planning for school, we'll see there are some different choices just as the ones Billie's thought of.

Pay Off the Credit Card in Nine Months

At present, Billie's Mastercard obligation isn't excessively high. However, the significant thing is that she needs to get out from under the steady intrigue installments. Once more, she's sensible enough to realize she can't afford just compensation the $2,800 she owes in one single amount; it will take some small installments spread over the more significant part of a year. Be that as it may, the considerable thing is she has an arrangement.

Resign from the Company at Age Fifty

Resigning at age fifty is likely ridiculous given her compensation and age, although this is an objective she can alter. Resigning at fifty methods, she has twelve and a half years before she can begin accepting Social Security benefits, so this may be somewhat tight. In any case, it's a decent spot to start from.

Spare Six Months of Income throughout the Next Twelve Years

At Eva's current pace of pay, this would add up to $24,624 after charges and before conclusions. This is a sensible entirety to save for crises, for example, medicinal issues, mishaps, or other startling occasions.

Stretch Goals

It's a smart thought to have a stretch objective—that is something you try to be that as it may, can accomplish by buckling down. Eva has such a yearning:

When she resigns, she needs to open a quaint little inn in a small beachfront town. B and Bs in comparable towns presently cost about $650,000 for the structure and activity, yet that cost will, without a doubt, ascend in the following twelve years. Then again, if Eva is fruitful, the B and B will likewise give a wellspring of salary during her retirement.

Understanding Your Current State

What Do You Have?

Before you can make a financial limit, you need to know everything about your budgetary circumstances. Even though you most likely comprehend when all is said about how much you spend and where you spend it, you might be stunned at how much you spend on specific things that don't appear they could include so quickly.

The procedure we will experience in the following parts is intended to give you an unflinchingly genuine examination of where you stand. If you tend to become overpowered effectively, keep a companion on backup whom you can telephone for help, and keep energetic music playing out of sight as you set up together your salary and costs.

What Counts as an Asset

We're going to begin by looking unbiasedly and smoothly at what you have — that is, your advantages. A benefit is basically whatever you possess. That can incorporate standard salary (for example, your check); incidental pay (for example, a legacy or an assessment bonus); your home, if you possess it; your vehicle, expecting you possess one; and all other material products that you claim. We're not recommending that you sell your home or your car—don't freeze— it's merely that it's essential to realize you're all out worth to make sense of instructions to understand your fantasies.

What doesn't consider a benefit is cash you can't depend on. Getting fortunate in the lottery this week doesn't pay since you could get nothing and be out the cost of a lottery ticket. The same thing is valid for something you will or may possess later on.

A few people contend about whether the cash you are owed should consider a benefit. I'm slanted to think not because you have no assurance of its being taken care of. At the point when the cash's quite your financial balance, I figure you can consider it a benefit, yet not up to that point.

Deciding Your Income

We'll focus first on your pay since that is the quickest and exact resource and the one that has the most prompt sway on your spending limit. Your pay incorporates any cash that comes into your ownership and can be depended on sooner rather than later. Your check is viewed as salary, yet the pay isn't constrained to a check you get from your manager—it is likewise an incapacity installment, a welfare check, a Social Security check, divorce settlement, youngster support, independent work salary from a private company, etc. Whatever cash comes in—cash that you can depend on—is the thing that you need to consider as salary.

Determine How Often You're Paid

In the first place, decide how frequently you are paid at work:

Week by week: Common for impermanent and provisional labor

Every other week: The most well-known way organizations pay their representatives— usually every other Friday.

Semimonthly: Often paid on the first and fifteenth of every month

Month to month: One check every month

Quarterly: Four times each year—this is uncommon

Semiannually: Twice per year—this is likewise uncommon

Every year: Almost incredible except if you're on a top managerial staff

In case you're paid on commission and aren't sure when your next check will be coming, audit your pay from a year ago and utilize that as a beginning stage. Assuming, in any case, something has changed since a year ago that may make you cause fewer deals this year to change in like manner. On the off chance that you get paid month to month (or even less now and again), you may have a more challenging time than most with your spending limit. The measure of your check may appear to be a great deal toward the start of the month; however, three or a month afterward, your costs may have surpassed that check. An exacting week by week spending limit can geniunely help.

Recognizing Your Sources of Income

You must recognize every one of your wellsprings of pay, include them up, and figure them on a yearly premise. In this worksheet, you calculate the entirety of your salary for a given payroll interval and increase it to get a yearly sum. Make sure to record the net measure of every check — that is, the sum you bring home after the assessments, protection, association contribution, and different things are deducted.

Your House as an Asset

Since we've got a decent image of your pay, how about we consider a portion of your different resources, we'll begin with your home, which is most likely the most important thing you possess. Note this possibly applies if you claim your home or apartment suite. On the off chance that you lease or have some other living circumstance, you can avoid the piece of this part follows.

Getting Equity

Value is the part of your home that you claim, contract-free. You can figure your value as follows:

1. Decide the present estimation of your home. This sum might be higher, and now and again, a lot higher than the sum you paid for it. The worth may likewise be lower than

what you paid if the house was exaggerated when you got it or if the land advertises in your territory has drooped. A home loan organization requires an examination, done by an expert, to decide this worth; however, you can figure, in light of what homes in your neighborhood have been selling for.

2. Check real estate professional locales and the paper to get a rundown of houses in your region and their asking costs. At that point, make an equivalency to your own home, utilizing places with an equivalent area, number of rooms, and size. You don't need to be definite; this gives you a rough approximation, so you realize what you're working with.

3. Decide the present result on your home loan. If you don't get a month to month articulation or receipt that discloses to you the resulting sum, call your home loan organization and request it.

4. Subtract the result from the present worth. This is the value of your home. Instead of computing your home's current estimation, a few loan specialists utilize the incentive from when you purchased the home. On the off chance that that was more than a couple of years prior, the present worth might be a lot higher (even though it likewise might be lower, contingent upon how lodging costs in your neighborhood have performed).

What Are You Spending?

Salary and resources are just a large portion of the condition in your financial limit. Presently you need to handle your spending. An expression of alert here: Some individuals are enticed, while making a financial limit, to fudge their spending numbers apiece. It very well may be humiliating when you understand the amount you're spending, consistently eating out or heading out to motion pictures. Be that as it may, it's significant in the accompanying worksheets that you are fair with yourself about the amount you spend and what you spend it on. Try not to stress about putting it down in high contrast. You don't need to demonstrate it to others if you would prefer not to. You need it to make a cautious, what's more, genuine assessment of your active assets. If you don't care for where you're going through cash ... well, I can tell you the best way to fix that.

You have two different ways to free up cash for your money related objectives: making more or spending less. Neither one of the ones is superior to the next, isn't that so?

Wrong! On the off chance that 18 percent of your pay goes to state and government charges, at that point, for each extra $1 you procure, you can utilize just eighty-two pennies to pay off obligation or put something aside for what's to come. Be that as it may, on the off chance that you can spare $1 of your costs, you can apply every last bit of it to your obligation or put it into reserve funds or ventures.

Dr. T. Anderson

TIP

See if your boss offers direct deposit, a component wherein your check is saved quickly into your financial balance. Rather than a check, you get a notification from your boss that the deposit has been made. You're bound to spare than spend if you utilize this element.

What Are You Spending Every Day?

The strategy for totaling your costs on Worksheet 4-1 is basic: You either report what you spent a week ago—step by step, cost by cost — or start new this week and record each use in the future. Utilize one worksheet consistently. If you record your expenses this coming week, be certain you don't attempt to be "acceptable" and spend not precisely what you generally do.

Screen Your Monthly Expenses

What Are Your Monthly Expenses?

Having taken a gander at your week after week spending designs, how about we proceed onward to those costs that happen on a month to month premise. Recording your month to month costs in your budget worksheet onlu like your day by day ones. In contrast, day by day costs are regularly money consumptions that you may overlook, month to month costs, for example, lease and utilities are bound to be paid with a money order or electronic exchange. For these month to month worksheets, you'll need to revisit your receipts, checkbook register, and bank explanations and utilize your memory. On the off chance that, then again, you record all your month to month costs beginning in January, you'll comprehend your January costs on January 31. Yet, you won't have an away from of your December going through until in 12 months, and that is significant time that you could use to arrive at your money related objectives rather than straying into the red. Instead, to all the more rapidly get a reasonable image of your month to month costs, uncover your bank articulations, checkbook register, receipts, etc. On the off chance that you utilize internet banking, go back through the electronic register of your exchanges.

Organizing Which Items You Want to Spend Cash On

You should now have a rundown of your costs by classification, with a need appended to everyone. On the off chance that you have enough pay to arrive at all of your budgetary objectives and still go through cash how you right now do, you won't require this organized rundown. Nonetheless, you can't meet your budgetary objectives on the off chance that you keep on spending in this example. (Recall Eva's understanding, illustrated in the previous segment.) If that is the situation, utilize this rundown to pick the regions that you totally would prefer not to cut back on (these are the things that have a need rating of 5). On the off chance that you have an excessive number of things with a high need to meet your money related objectives, sub-prioritize those things, so you concoct only a couple. Spending on these things will make every one of the reductions simpler to swallow. Recollect that you are the one in particular who can decide your needs on the off chance that you would prefer to drive an old vehicle with the goal that you can, in any case, bear to purchase natural products of the soil, do it. Recollect Likewise, while you're settling on these hard decisions, that your objective here isn't to make your life less agreeable. Instead, it's to discover a way of understanding your fantasies. Such a practice may expect you to make a few forfeits in the present all together to arrive at your objectives later on.

Intermittent Splurges

So does keeping to spending mean you can never go out for supper again or then again spend a sentimental end of the week in a pleasant retreat inn? No, not. It just implies that you have a spending plan for these things. At the point when you're following your costs, search for these sorts of "binge spend" things. What amount have you been spending on them? Expecting you need to keep on doing so, search for approaches to overdo it yet without fundamentally going through as a lot of cash.

There's nothing amiss with going through cash to live it up—given this is the thing that you need to do and that you've remembered it for your financial limit.

Putting Income and Financial Obligations Together

The accompanying worksheet is one of the most significant instruments for pinpointing why any budgetary difficulties exist for you. If you have more commitments than salary (which means you're most likely in or near paying off debtors), or on the other hand, on the off chance that you have more salary than commitments (which is the initial step toward a more advantageous money related picture).

Recognizing Potential Cash-Flow Problems

Frequently, suppose your pay marginally surpasses your commitments on paper. In that case, you seem as though you'll get by fine and dandy, however as a general rule, you may get yourself missing the mark at specific occasions of the year.

For instance, Assume that you have a payment of $26,000 every year (after charges) and $25,000 in commitments. An issue frequently emerges when one of your occasional costs, for example, vehicle protection, is expected. You may have enough pay from January to December to cover your vehicle protection; however, if your protection bill lands in February, you may not have had the opportunity to place enough cash into investment funds every month to cover this cost. This is known as an income issue. To oversee this circumstance effectively, you need to pay off your obligation (or increment your pay) to where you're living far enough beneath your pay that you don't experience difficulty paying your occasional huge costs.

Enjoy a Reprieve If You Need It

If your monetary picture is relatively depressing, this section may have been challenging for you. The following passage, which tells you the best way to build up composed spending that you will be living with for the following, not many months and years, most likely won't be any simpler. Regardless of whether you're the sort who likes to drive through one part to the following, you may need to take a break for a couple of hours or medium-term. Try not to surrender here, however! Enjoy a short reprieve, breathe in profoundly, and prepare to change your life to improve things.

Presently you are prepared to make a spending limit.

The explanation you make a spending limit is because you have money related objectives. These may run from disposing of obligation because of hospital expenses to putting something aside for retirement to purchasing your first house; regardless of your money-related circumstance, you have budgetary objectives, although you may not consider them that way. On the off chance that you have a specific way of life you need to live, places you need to go, or individuals you need to enable, you have budgetary objectives.

These monetary objectives are the instruments you will use to construct your bigger life objectives. For specific individuals, financial goals are finishes in themselves. However, for a large portion of us, we need to utilize our accounts to accomplish something—regardless of whether it's to resign and run a B and B like Eva or something different.

At the point when you make a spending limit, you keep the entirety of your monetary objectives as the focal center, making sense of how to cut your current costs—or increment your present pay—to get you on track to meet those objectives. How you choose to curtail or include payment will be as one of a kind as your goals seem to be. You may settle on altogether different decisions than your neighbors do about how, how well, and where you'll live. Each choice you cause will be explicit to your monetary objectives and your current budgetary circumstance, which nobody else needs to think about or concur with. On the off chance that others question your choices, grin! They don't have similar objectives you do, and you know you're destined for success in accomplishing your fantasies. Remember, however, that you will most likely be unable to meet all of your objectives if you additionally need to keep up your present degree of spending. (Recall that Eva required to change both her general goals and her ways of managing money to get where she needed to be.) Planning is frequently the craft of bargain: You need to choose what to surrender to get what you need.

when a Deal Is Not a Deal

To keep afloat monetarily, you need to spend short of what you make. This fundamental point is the most significant standard for building and living inside a spending limit. You basically can't meet money related objectives if you try not to live inside your methods.

However, numerous Americans spend more than they make, and it regularly begins with only a couple of terrible choices. Here's a model. A couple of years prior, a money related guide on TV said that insofar as loan costs on new vehicles remained at 0 or 1 percent (which vehicle organizations were offering at that time), the best monetary speculation an individual could make would be to purchase another vehicle. The council recommended that you'd be insane not to exploit this circumstance.

Presently envision somebody watching that program who claimed a five-year-old vehicle paid off and ran fine; however, hearing that money related guidance, our vehicle proprietor chose to go out and purchase another vehicle. The open door for financing this low may never return. Along these lines, the vehicle proprietor exchanges the flawlessly fine car and gets a lot on another vehicle. In any case, after two months, the vehicle proprietor starts to feel the squeeze. Month to month vehicle installments go from $0 (on the old vehicle) to $318, and protection costs go up to $168 every year. Previously, our vehicle purchasing companion continuously had a touch of additional cash each month—enough to put $200 in investment funds and still have somewhat left finished. In any case, presently, there's nothing to go into investment funds and no additional money around. Even in the initial scarcely any months, the vehicle proprietor is starting to put a couple of food supplies on the charge card to get by. In a little while, this one blameless buy has prompted a spiraling budgetary issue. The vehicle was not the best speculation our vehicle proprietor could have made. A better choice would have been not to consider getting a new car until the former had a huge issue. The drop in intrigue rates set aside our vehicle proprietor cash; however, the vehicle itself—at that specific time—was something our companion didn't need or plan for. Keep in mind: An item is just a decent arrangement on the off chance that you've gotten ready for it and can bear the cost of it inside the setting of your other money related objectives. Nothing— not low loan costs, a deal on shoes, the place you had always wanted—is ever a decent arrangement on the off chance that it expects you to spend more than you make.

Spend Money Only on Budgeted Items

After you set up a financial limit, you can go through cash just on what your spending says you can burn through cash on, which drives the vast majority insane! They feel as if another person is controlling their lives or that they're living in a straitjacket. In any case, while spending plans can be choking, the main power controlling your spending is you—or, to be increasingly accurate, your fiscal objectives. Assume your essential budgetary objective is to take a two-month excursion to Europe. You're certain that you need to do this, and your spending limit reflects it. Since you'll be taking time off work without pay, you're sparing for the excursion as well as for the salary you'll miss while you're gone. You've made sense of that if you surrender your biscotti and espresso each morning, turn down your indoor regulator, and quit purchasing garments for a year, you'll have the option to do it. Be that as it may, a few months into the year, you conclude that this "insane" spending plan won't disclose to you how to run your life and that nobody should live without biscotti and espresso in a less-than-warm house while wearing old garments.

What precisely has occurred here? Fundamentally, your momentary money related objectives have a higher need than the more extended term objective of needing to go to Europe. Along these lines, the monetary allowance must be adjusted to mirror those money related objectives, provided that biscotti and garments aren't in the financial limit; you can't burn through cash on them and still make it to Europe. To spend euros in about a year, you can't purchase things since you've consented to surrender.

Save for unforeseen expenses

Individuals frequently stumble into budgetary difficulty since they don't expect the unforeseen. By deliberately putting something aside for sudden costs, you can break this cycle. A sudden cost might be a car collision that expects you to pay your deductible or a fix to your home. A crisis can even be an arranged cost that comes due before you anticipate it. For instance, assume you intended to get away not long from now. Out of the blue, your closest companion is going to a meeting in the Bahamas; also, requests that you come, remain for nothing in the lodging and pay just airfare, furthermore, nourishment. You conclude that presently is a superior time to take an economical get-away. In any case, given your objective to get out and avoid obligation, you try not to set output the stumble on Visas. This outing will be a lot simpler choice for you because you have cash in the bank to get against. In a perfect world, you should keep a half year's salary in the bank. On the off chance that there are two breadwinners in your family, keep a half year of every individual's salary in reserve funds. Indeed, this is a great deal of cash, yet a lot of cash makes decisions throughout your life. You're never going to feel stuck again: If you're laid off, you have the opportunity to get a new line of work you truly need; if you've been searching for another house and locate the ideal one, yet the ebb and flow proprietors won't sit tight for you to sell yours first, you can utilize your reserve funds as an initial installment, supplanting the investment funds after you sell your current house.

The secret to having cash accessible for surprising costs is two-fold. In the first place, you never dunk into your investment funds except if you're confronted with a genuinely one of a kind circumstance. A shoe deal at your preferred retail chain is not a particular circumstance. What's more, if you have the opportunity to get ready for a sudden occasion, spare ahead of time by changing your way of life to free up more cash for reserve funds, yet don't dunk into your investment funds except if you have to. The money in your bank account is for that gracious my-gosh-what-am-I going-to-do-now circumstance. The second piece of the secret to keeping reserve funds close by for unforeseen occasions is consistently to supplant it after you use it. On the off chance that you have six months' pay in the bank and you utilize one month's compensation to make up the distinction between your inability pay and your typical compensation, when you return to work all day, promptly start supplanting that one month's compensation. These two ideas—leaving cash in investment funds for sudden costs and supplanting any money that you acquire from your investment funds at the point when startling circumstances emerge—are not fundamental in our general public. You'll find that most Americans don't believe they're able to do this. On the off chance that they see they have cash in the bank, they'll spend it on whatever they think will improve their lives right then and there. Be that as it may, the truth, having this security enables you to pick, and that is the best force you'll ever have—a lot more prominent than the big-screen Television for the Super Bowl.

Dr. T. Anderson

Returning to Your Goals and Priorities

As you experience the planning procedure, you may wind up amending your extended haul budgetary objectives and your shorter-term spending needs. This amending doesn't make you an awful individual! It's merely the truth of everybody's circumstance: We each have a set pay, and our wants to spend surpass our pay.

Assume, for instance, that you have the accompanying objectives: Save for a little upfront installment on the house in a half year; purchase new furniture for your home when you move in; and inside two years, increment investment funds so that it rises to a half year of salary. You additionally have your eye on purchasing another vehicle in a year, and you've, as of late, added this to your rundown of objectives. Assume that with your present salary, you spend all that you make. Indeed, to spare $10,000 for an upfront installment on the house in a half year, you're going to need to spare nearly $1,700 every month. The furniture will cost $500 for a half-year; sparing a half year's compensation will require $900 every month for a long time, and the new vehicle, less the exchange on your current vehicle, will take $1,200 every month for a year. Through and through, this is nearly $4,300 per month. Except if you're as of now living an unimaginably extravagant way of life, the possibility of having the option to remove $4,300 of your present going through to discover this cash is thin. You have two alternatives. You can figure out how to get more cash-flow by finding a second line of work, doing independent work, beginning your own low maintenance business, staying at work past 40 hours, or getting another line of work that pays more cash. That is one approach to meet your objectives, yet remember that at whatever point you work more hours, you quit any trace of something valuable—time. On the off chance that you have the opportunity to spend, if you intend to work the additional hours as it were for a brief timeframe, and if working more hours won't risk your wellbeing, unleash devastation on your association with your children or life partner, or the other hand, remove you from a leisure activity that you love, maybe it will be alright.

Be that as it may, on the off chance that you need to focus on this way of life for a long time, you may discover it unsuitable. The other choice is to return and return to your spending needs and money related objectives. Regardless of whether you've cut your costs as much as you might suspect you can, perhaps you can, at present, cut back some more. Regardless of whether one of your spending needs is to have the option to chat on the telephone for a boundless measure of time with long-separation companions and family members, maybe you could talk during the free end of the week minutes or change to email some portion of the time. Or on the other hand, you may conclude that because your money related objectives are very significant, you're willing to surrender this cost, regardless of whether you've recently concluded that it was a high need.

Then again, you may decide to reconsider your objectives, to look for changes there. Maybe, for instance, you choose to purchase the house in four years rather than a half year, which gives you considerably more time to put something aside for the initial installment and the furnishings. Maybe, because both the house and the telephone calls are sufficiently significant, you can manage your current vehicle for a few additional years. Perhaps you continue working toward getting a half year's pay in the bank, yet stretch that objective out to ten years rather than two.

Make a Budget You Can Stick To

On the off chance that you haven't yet recorded your objectives, you should begin there. On a bit of paper or a spreadsheet, make a rundown of them. You'll have to know your objectives before you can build up a spending limit.

Impediments to Reaching Financial Goals

En route, you'll get familiar with the snags that forestall numerous individuals from arriving at their money related objectives: charges, expansion, passing and inability, absence of an arrangement, sense of self, and spillage. Government and state charges are said to be one of life's two surenesses, and they're about consistently on the ascent. Luckily, there are approaches to limit the assessments you pay.

Expansion consumes salary. The individuals who don't get ready for it can end up short of what they need. Expansion is one of the scalawags that can get individuals into budgetary difficulty before they understand it. Indeed, even a small sum of swelling after some time can influence your way of life on the off chance that you don't design appropriately. Predictable arranging and sparing can assist you with remaining in front of expansion. Albeit nobody likes to discuss them, demise and handicap can be destroying to a family that has not made arrangements for these occasions. You may have bequest plans, and you ought to have a will. Alone, be that as it may, these are insufficient. What might your monetary circumstance be if an inability constrained you to stop work for a considerable length of time, years, or maybe a great remainder?

How might you adapt as you watch your vehicle being repossessed? How okay feel if your companion needed to maintain two sources of income? Many think that it's awkward or even agonizing to talk or consider these things; however, you should. You will figure out how to anticipate demise and incapacity, giving you a more prominent conviction that all is good than you have now. I've just referenced that numerous individuals respond to budgetary occasions as they occur, rather than making a bound together arrangement for arriving at their objectives. Without an arrangement, you'll have a much lower possibility of progress. Inner self is the hardest hindrance to survival. A few people can't reach their monetary objectives because their self-images disrupt the general flow. They purchase vehicles also, join clubs to intrigue individuals. They live in houses they can't manage.

Rather than making arrangements for the future, they stay aware of the Joneses today, a choice that shields them from arriving at monetary freedom. I'll appear you what occurs on the off chance that you increment your way of life one year too early. You'll be stunned by the distinction one year can make in whether you reach your objectives. Spillage can be a shrouded impediment among you and your money related objectives. Spillage happens when you don't reinvest your venture income to assist you with meeting your goal. Did you spend your last stock profit rather than contributing it? That is a spillage, and it can geniunely include after some time.

On the off chance that you spare $5,000 per year and win 10 percent every year, you would acquire $500 the primary year. It's so natural to spend that 500 on prompt needs furthermore, needs. If you do that, following 20 years, you will have the cash you put in: $100,000. In any case, on the off chance that you reinvest the premium consistently, you'll have $286,375. Are those new garments or golf clubs worth a distinction of more than $186,000? Spillage likewise happens when you pick a self-assertive dollar sum as an objective; however, damage your objective by going through a piece of that cash. For instance, you figure things would be extraordinary if you had $30,000. At the point when you've spared $30,000, you celebrate with a get-away that expenses $5,000, leaving you with just $25,000. You can work back to $30,000, yet an absence of order has cost you time and compound intrigue. To dodge spillage, you should treat the cash you are sparing, what's more, contributing as distant for any reason other than your objective. Else, you disintegrate your retirement fund. Try not to spend the school investment funds on a new vehicle.

4
BUILDING A SUCCESSFUL BUSINESS

What is an effective business?

There are numerous approaches to measure the achievement of a business. Sadly a large number of them depend absolutely on financial measures. I experience a ton of business administrators who are amazingly hard on themselves. Since their business may be experiencing an extreme time, they accuse themselves and begin to build up the inclination that they are disappointed at what they do.

I might want to accept this opportunity to have my state on what makes a business fruitful. To start with, the way an individual is set up to move out of a safe place to face a challenge and put their neck on the money related slashing square makes them a triumph. Having a week after week pay bundle would be the best inclination for most business administrators who will, in general, battle from the everyday. I recall when I began my first business. I was 18 years old, and I had times when I needed more cash to put petroleum in the vehicle to return home, so I dozed in the shop—some of the time for seven days one after another. I am doing whatever it takes not to be a saint, yet I am demonstrating the level of commitment that numerous business administrators have.

Secondly, I am continually dazzled by the nature of administration and the items created by a private company. I am sure that a few people must believe that little, one-individual organizations couldn't in any way, shape, or form make any items or offer any administrations of world-class quality. I differ totally, and I see proof of this reality consistently. There are some extraordinarily capable and committed individuals out there who are making progress toward greatness in manners that the world's most prominent organizations would never envision.

At long last, the level of constancy that I see from numerous independent company administrators continually astonishes me. I have had individuals come to me who have lost everything at the time of 60, and they need some advertising counsel on their next adventure. They grin; they are confident, and they are savvy. Independent venture administrators are regularly humiliated to state that they are having money related troubles. I attempt to clarify that there wouldn't be a business on the planet that hasn't experienced income issues eventually, so try not to pound yourself since you are making some extreme memories.

There are numerous different approaches to gauge achievement separated from simply money related outcomes. Achievement is accomplished by having extraordinary items, offering excellent help, having a definite affinity with your staff, and knowing inside yourself that you have worked admirably.

GETTING INTO THE RIGHT BUSINESS

Achievement in a specific business depends on having in a well-created state the resources required in that business. Without a tremendous melodic workforce, nobody can succeed as an instructor of music. Without excellent mechanical capacities, nobody can make incredible progress in any of the mechanical exchanges. Without respect and pizazz for business, nobody can prevail in trade interests. In any case, to have in a well-created express the resources required in your specific work does not guarantee riches. Some artists have a fantastic ability, and who yet stay poor. Some metalworkers and woodworkers have a remarkable mechanical capacity, yet they don't get rich. What's more, there are vendors with acceptable abilities for managing individuals who fall flat.

The various resources are devices. It is essential to have fantastic apparatuses, yet it is likewise fundamental that the instruments should be utilized rightly. One man can take a sharply observed, a square, and a decent plane and manufacture an attractive article of furniture. Another man can take similar apparatuses and set to work to copy the article; in any case, his generation will be a bungle. He doesn't have a clue step by step instructions to utilize great apparatuses fruitfully. The different resources of your psyche are the devices you should take the steps needed to make you wealthy. It will be simpler for you to succeed on the off chance that you get into a business for which you are well-prepared with mental apparatuses. As a rule, you will do best in that business that will utilize your most grounded resources, the one for which you usually are "best fitted." But there are additional restrictions to this announcement. Nobody ought to see his livelihood as being unavoidably fixed by the abilities with which he was conceived.

You can get wealthy in any business if you have not the correct ability for it; you can build up that ability. It only implies that you should make your devices as you come, rather than binding yourself to the utilization of those with which you were conceived. It will be simpler for you to prevail in a work for which you now have the gifts in a well-created state. Be that as it may, you can prevail in any business since you can build up any simple ability, and there is no ability of which you have not, in any event, a modest quantity. You will get rich most effectively if you do that for which you are best fitted. Be that as it may, you will get rich most acceptably on the off chance you do what you need to do.

Doing what you need to do is life. What's more, there is no genuine fulfillment in living if we are constrained to do something which we don't care to do and neglect to do what we need to do.

The longing to play music is a force looking for articulation and advancement. The longing to imagine mechanical gadgets is additionally a force looking for articulation and refinement. Where there is no force either created or lacking to do something, there will never be any longing to do that thing. Where there is a powerful urge to do a thing, it is confirmation that the ability to do it is solid; what's more, it just should be created and applied in the right way.

Considering everything, it is ideal to choose a business for which you have the best-created ability. Be that as it may, if you want to participate in a specific profession, you should select that work as a definitive objective. Since you can, would what you like to, it is your right and benefit to engage in the business or side interest which will be generally harmonious and lovely. You are not obliged to do what you don't care to do and ought not to do it aside from as a way to bring you to your ideal work. If there are past slip-ups whose results have put you in a bothersome business or condition, you might be obliged for quite a while to do what you try not to get a kick out of the chance to do. Be that as it may, you can make it's doing wonderful by realizing that it is making it workable to go to your ideal work.

If you feel that you are not in the correct employment, try not to act too hurriedly to get into another one. The ideal way, by and large, to change a business or a domain is by development. Try not to be reluctant to make an unexpected and radical change if the open door is introduced and on the off chance that you feel after cautious thought that it is the correct chance. However, never make an unexpected or radical move when you are in question regarding the knowledge of doing as such. There will never be any rush on the inventive plane.

What's more, there is no absence of chance. When you escape the serious personality, you will comprehend that you never need to act hurriedly. Nobody else is going to beat you to the thing you need to do. If one spot is taken, another, what's more, a superior one will be opened for you somewhat more distant on. There is a lot of time. At the point when you are in question, pause. It depends on the consideration of your vision and increments your confidence and reason.

What's more, definitely, in times of uncertainty and hesitation, develop an appreciation. A day or two spent in pondering the vision of what you need and decisively thanksgiving that you are getting it will bring your brain into such close association with the Infinite that you will make no botch when you do act. There is a mind that knows everything to know. Furthermore, on the off chance that you have a profound appreciation, you can come into close solidarity with this brain by confidence and the reason to progress throughout everyday life.

Slip-ups originate from acting quickly or from acting in dread or question or in the carelessness of the privilege rationale, which is more life to all and less to none. As you go on in a specific way, openings will come to you in expanding numbers. You will require to be exceptionally relentless in your confidence and reason and keep in close touch with the Supreme Power through respectful appreciation. Do all you can do in an ideal way every day, yet do it without flurry, stress, or dread. Go as quickly as you can, yet never rush. Recollect that at the time you start to hustle, you stop to be a maker and become a contender. You drop once more into the old plane once more. At whatever point you wind up hustling, stop.

Fix your consideration on the psychological picture of the thing you need and start to express gratefulness that you are getting it. This activity of appreciation will never neglect to fortify your confidence and reestablish your motivation. Ten significant hints for running a fruitful business. The accompanying focuses depend on my perceptions of fruitful business administrators. I accept that they are all similarly substantial.

1. Encircle yourself with constructive individuals and keep pessimism out of your life. On the off chance that you don't care for what you are doing, then begin wanting to change your business. It is stunning how a lot of cash you can make at the point when you love what you do.
2. On the off chance that you guarantee to accomplish something, at that point, ensure that you do it. Perhaps the most significant ruin of private companies is an absence of unwavering quality. The greatest commendation I can get from a customer is the point at which they recognize me for carrying out responsibility on schedule and spending plan.
3. Be sorted out. Set aside the effort to sort out those records, balance the checkbook, and clear the work area or clean the workshop. Working in a chaotic situation welcomes botch.
4. Invest wholeheartedly in your appearance. Iron those overalls, clean the workplace, and put a few blossoms in the lounge area— individuals notice. On the off chance that you look great, you will feel better, and your business will profit.

5. Praise individuals indeed—your family, your staff, what's more, your clients. On the off chance that you haven't got anything decent to state, sell up, and move away.
6. Treat everybody that strolls in the entryway as a potential client—regardless of whether they are attempting to sell you something, one day they might be hoping to purchase something too.
7. Try not to stress over the absence of cash—take a shot at profiting. Stressing over a bill never got it paid any quicker. Invest the energy executing some straightforward advertising thoughts and making sense of how to get more clients in the entryway.
8. Be available to new and creative thoughts. If you find yourself saying the feared words, 'that is the way we have constantly done it and that is how we are going to continue doing it,' maybe you are not as adaptable and open as you could be. A thought that could make you a great deal of cash might be in the leader of a companion or staff part who feels that you would not be open if they voiced their recommendation. Empower creative and open reasoning.
9. Be genuine and moral in each managing that you have. Significantly, you can walk down the road with your head held high.
10. Invest significant energy to unwind and energize your batteries. You try not to get an award on the off chance that you work relentlessly for a long time— you get solidified supply routes, ulcers, and a sore back. It's not about cash; it's tied in with requiring some investment for you. It is an

opportunity to eat well, make up for lost time with the companions that you are in every case too occupied even to consider seeing, toss the canine a Frisbee, see a motion picture, go angling or make up for lost time with missed rest.

Individuals by and large beginning an independent venture or purchase a little business for various reasons. It is then because they are acceptable at their picked calling and feel that they can bring home the bacon working for themselves. Once in a while, it is a way of life change, and once in a while, it is a deep-rooted dream. With the approach of conservation and repetition bundles or early retirement payouts, there are a lot more individuals confronting retirement well before they are prepared. They have money, and they have the vitality and energy to begin their own business. The issue is that they seldom have the experience required to run their new pursuit and to profit.

Maintaining a business requires numerous abilities that require significant investment to create. The inquiry is how a lot of time do you need to create them? We are regularly reminded that numerous independent companies come up short inside the initial hardly any years. From my experience, the two fundamental reasons are an absence of beginning capital (insufficient cash) and an absence of promoting capacity. The individuals running these organizations buckle down, by and large, have fantastic items, and regularly are committed to making their business a triumph; however, they don't have the foggiest idea how to find new clients or continue existing ones.

So, where do you turn for advertising guidance? You can connect with the administrations of an advertising expert to help create expert advertising plans and give you a bounty of thoughts and recommendations on drawing in more business. This is the thing that a great many advertising specialists, including myself, do the world over consistently. By and large, our customers are more significant firms with the monetary allowance to bring in pro exhortation.

Notwithstanding, most by far of organizations are little one or two-person activities that have exceptionally restricted assets. They can't bear to have their promoting specialist accessible if the need arises. Their needs are progressively prompt, and their support, including time and cash, are commonly constrained. The advantage to this is a large portion of these independent ventures ordinarily need a delicate bump the correct way to deliver sensational upgrades in their business. Based on this need, I chose to compose this book. My fantasy was to make an unmistakable, simple to-peruse manual that any business administrator could get and begin utilzing right away.

I needed to offer a lot of straightforward advertising thoughts that were attempted and tried. They must be coherent, simple to execute furthermore, reasonable. The thoughts and methodologies recommended don't require any uncommon aptitudes, and they won't take up a great deal of your time. Business administrators need to have the opportunity to do things straight away, not anticipate ten years. On the off chance that business hushes up, they need to have the option to take care of business right away. This book will give you the chance to be proactive about showcasing today. Showcasing thoughts is significant for progress; in any case, I accept that having the correct frame of mind is basic. I have been sufficiently lucky to work with a great deal of extremely fruitful business administrators. They all have comparable frames of mind and considerations on working together, and I accept that is what sets them separated from those organizations that consistently appear to battle. I have included numerous proposals that depend on my perceptions of these exceptionally useful business administrators. If the thoughts and proposals, point by point, help only one business quit battling and get fruitful, I will be an extremely glad man.

The Five Deadly Business Sins

Drucker remarked that there is nobody equation for business accomplishment since every business and industry is extraordinary. Every business needs arrangements and procedures suitable for that business yet, Five Deadly Business Sins should have stayed away from. If any of these wrongdoings are submitted, it can have sad consequences for the company.

Sin One: Worship of High-Profit Margins and Premium Prices

Sin Two: Charging for New Products What the Market Will Bear

Sin Three: Cost - Driven Pricing versus Cost - Driven Costing

Sin Four: Killing Tomorrow's Opportunities on the Altar of Yesterday

Sin Five: Feeding Problems and Starving Opportunities

Dr. T. Anderson

Sin 1: Worship of High-Profit Margins and Premium Prices

The love of the high-profit edge is in this manner, not just a hazardous error — it is venerating a bogus god. As per Drucker, " Profit isn't equivalent to overall revenue. The benefit is edge increased by the turnover of capital. Subsequently, most extreme profitability and greatest benefit stream are gotten by the profit edge that creates the ideal market standing with the ideal turnover of capital." (Note that Drucker did not characterize "ideal.") Drucker likewise noticed that one reason for this issue is that a high-profit edge is a bookkeeping hallucination. His view was that such intuition takes a gander at the expense of making an item yet doesn't mull over the expense of selling or overhauling it, even though these expenses usually are a lot higher for high - edge items than for low-edge items. Roger Best's idea of Net Marketing Contribution will, in general, help Drucker's sees here. As per Drucker, the love of high net revenues presents an open door for the rivalry to assume control over the market. Coming up next are two instances of this.

Sin 2: Charging for New Products What the Market Will Bear

The correct method for valuing another item or administration is to value it right away at the value it should be sold three years; consequently, when its costs have fallen. This implies that not harvesting colossal benefits the initial barely any years. It might even mean a real misfortune for the principal year or, on the other hand, so. This wrongdoing is firmly identified with the first—endeavoring to value another item at what the market will bear. As per Drucker, the right arrangement to value another item depends on the expectation to learn and adapt.

The expectation to absorb information idea is that the expense of assembling another item will diminish as the business acquires experience in assembling it. Drucker indicated that it isn't uncommon for these expenses to diminish by more than 40 percent within three years. Along these lines, within three years after another item is presented, the costs of assembling the item will be practically 50% of what they were at the point at which it was first introduced. Technique specialists Peter Read also, Harold Kerzner attributes this decrease in expenses to the accompanying elements:

- Work efficiency (generally significant)
- Work specialization and strategies improvement (task specialization: Taylor's Scientific Management)
- New generation forms
- Showing signs of improvement execution from generation gear (expanded yield: for example, the limit of a liquid synergist splitting unit develops typically around 50 percent over the course of ten years)
- Changes in the asset blend (more affordable assets utilised after some time: low talented work replaces costly work, computerisation, and so forth.)
- Item institutionalisation
- Item update

- Motivators and disincentives (compensation)

Drucker upheld that the new item should be at first evaluated at what it would need to be sold for inside three years as a feasible aftereffect of new serious, or substitute, items being sold at lower costs. This underlying valuing technique, he felt, makes it difficult for contenders and substitute items to enter the market.

Sin 3: Cost - Driven Pricing versus Cost - Driven Costing

Clients don't consider it to be their business to guarantee that makers make a profit. Organizations submit the cost-driven estimating sin by totaling costs and adding a benefit to land at a price to be charged the client. Interestingly, cost-driven costing plans the item or administration. The accompanying models represent each approach.

Case: Cost - Driven Pricing Example:

Control Data versus IBM

When PCs got famous in the mid-1960s, Control Data had what was viewed as the world's most exceptional PC. The value it landed at for the PC at the time was the assembling costs in addition to a benefit. The outcome was that the PC was excessively costly for most clients, and albeit potential clients yielded it was the best PC accessible — deals didn't emerge. IBM then again posed the inquiry What is the business client ready to pay for a computer?14 It planned a PC that was the second rate compared to Control Data's. Yet, it was evaluated utilizing the Price-Driven Costing Approach, and the rest is history in terms of where the two organizations are today.

Sin 4: Killing Tomorrow's Opportunities on the Altar of Yesterday

By 2020 or thereabouts, it's sensibly sure that the enduring organizations will be those that didn't submit the transgression of butchering on the special raised area of recently the new chance—that is internet business, regardless of whether business to - business or business - to - consumer. Organizations frequently endeavor to keep and support present items when they believe they have a couple of good years left, even though deals are declining and client inclinations and the market evolve. Drucker talked about this in his idea of Planned.

Relinquishment — when to forsake an item and present new items. Because of endeavoring to save yesterday, open doors for tomorrow are lost. Drucker additionally contended that frequently the best performing individuals in the association are allocated to such issues instead of concentrating on circumstances.

Case: Price-Driven Costing Example: Henry Ford

Numerous antiquarians credit Henry Ford for designing the sequential construction system to make the Model T Ford that sold for $500. In reality, Henry Ford was one of the first to utilize the Price-Driven Costing Approach. He asked, "What is the value the normal client is happy to pay for a basic vehicle that came in one shading, dark?" His advertising examination reasoned that $500 was the correct value, still high in those days, and he consequently educated his designers to decide how they could fabricate the auto and make a benefit selling it for $ 500.15

Sin 5: Feeding Problems and Starving Opportunities

The fourth and fifth sins are firmly related. Fundamentally Sin 5 arrangements to protect Yesterday and overlooking Tomorrow, yet from a slightly alternate point of view. This issue is intensified by the association's revealing framework that spotlights issues and where targets are not being met, typically on the first page of the week after week or month to month the board report. Open doors for the association to seek after are not recorded here and, whenever recorded by any means, are covered in the report.

Drucker remarked that better-performing associations allocate their best individuals to seeking after open doors for development. They moreover have two pages to their administration reports, the typical issues, what's more, status page, and an Opportunity page. Drucker had kept on worrying throughout the years that associations that don't advance won't endure. In this manner, identifying chances and relegating assets (development spending plan and top-performing individuals) are essential to the association's endurance.

Subside Drucker exhorted that these Five Deadly Business Sins need to be maintained a strategic distance from a business to endure and develop. The key take-aways from this section manage two issues:

1. Estimating Strategies: What is the most fitting procedure for the presentation of another item? Drucker recommends Price-Based Costing and Learning Curve Pricing.
2. Development.

Concerning valuing, Drucker's Learning Curve Pricing is one technique an association can consider, contingent upon various factors. Kotler developed Drucker's dangerous sins by recommending there are different errors settled on in valuing choices. He delineated these as follows:

1. Estimating is too cost - arranged.
2. Cost isn't overhauled regularly enough to profit by showcase changes.
3. Cost is set free of the showcasing blend instead of as a natural component of the market-situating system.
4. Cost isn't shifted enough for various item things, showcase fragments, dispersion channels, and buy occasions. Kotler likewise points by the point the means that are essential in setting up a cost.

These means include:

- Choosing the evaluating objective
- Deciding interest
- Assessing costs
- Breaking down contenders' costs, costs, and offers
- Choosing a valuing strategy
- Choosing the last price

As indicated by Kotler, estimating targets can differ from essentially having the option to make due as a business right to picking up product quality authority. He arranged five evaluating objectives:

1. Endurance: Applies to the firm confronted with overcapacity, extraordinary challenge, or changing client needs. On the off chance that the cost can cover variable and fixed costs, the organization can remain in business. He considered this a momentary procedure, and if the firm can't inevitably include esteem, it will confront elimination.
2. Amplify Current Profits: Maximize current benefit, income, or pace of degree of profitability. This methodology expects the firm can decide request and cost capacities. By underlining recent execution, it might forfeit since a long time ago runs execution by disregarding impacts of other advertising blend factors, for example, contenders' responses, or lawful limitations on cost.
3. Expand Market Share: Some accept a higher deal volume compares to bring down unit expenses and, in this manner, higher since quite a while ago run benefits. The procedure is to set the most reduced value accepting the market is value touchy (versatile). Texas Instruments (TI) rehearses Market - Penetration Pricing: it assembles an enormous plant, sets a low cost to pick up a piece of the pie, and brings down the value once more (expectation to absorb information impacts). This system demoralizes

rivalry from entering the market, as was depicted by Drucker.

4. Market Skimming: Applies to organizations presenting innovation. One model is Sony and the principal superior quality TV: the value was $46,000 in 1990 when presented initially, in 1993 value declined significantly to $8,000, and in 2001 the value plunged to $3,000. An individual model was buying an HP mini-computer for $500 to use for my Pepperdine College MBA courses in the mid–the 1970s. About 40 years after the fact, a number cruncher can play out the equivalent, and significantly, a more significant number of capacities can be obtained for under $5. Kotler proposes that Market Skimming works when there are sufficient purchasers and high current interest. The unit cost of delivering little volume is not very high, the high starting cost doesn't pull in more contenders to the market, and the significant expense imparts a picture of a prevalent item. This methodology is identified with Drucker's wrongdoing of Charging What the Market Will Bear.

5. Item - Quality Leadership: This procedure endeavors to sell esteem; what's more, different highlights persuade clients that the item is worth the additional cost. For instance, Xerox's evaluation, when contrasted with the challenge when it was first presented in the late 1950s, concentrated on the utilization of plain versus covered paper and the mix of duplicate quality and usability contrasted with existing covered paper duplicates. Additionally, the underlying procedure of charging by the

replication as opposed to purchasing the copier (which Xerox would not at first do) was a one of a kind methodology that permitted the organization to at first accomplish this goal. As per Roger Best, various Cost-Based and MarketBased evaluating techniques rely upon where the item is in its lifecycle. Cost-Based estimating methodologies run from Floor Pricing to Harvest Pricing, while Market-Based methodologies extend from Skim Evaluating to Plus One Pricing.

The idea of " flexibility " additionally should be considered in deciding value (Kotler's subsequent advance). The utilization of " packaging " and " unbundling " as evaluating methodologies, just as the effect of cannibalization brought about by the presentation of new items, was dismissed in Drucker's talks and made further Gaps need to be shut. A nitty gritty discourse of these procedures and other valuing contemplations is excluded here, yet many promoting books can close these Gaps. Advance your business from the outside in Be glad to advance your business by putting a sign on the divider. I managed an enormous visual communication organization with an upstairs office on probably the busiest crossing point around. They had a vast divider in full view from anyplace on the convergence, and they never got around to painting a sign on this divider. In the long run, they moved out since the business was awful. On the off chance that they had put in a couple of hundred dollars on an essential sign, the business would have an entire part better a mess quicker.

Open-air signage works seven days every week, 24 hours a day, regardless of whether you are open or shut. Use it to its full advantage. Know about neighborhood government guidelines administering signage limitations, for example, size. Work with these guidelines, yet make your signs as large as you legitimately can. Try not to miss them, only a couple of words laying out what you do and when you are open. Make the hues stick out also, check any work of art altogether for spelling or syntactic errors. I once had a SCUBA Diving school, one day I put a sham on the rooftop wearing old plunging hardware, and it looked genuine. The measure of inclusion and introduction that this sham gave my business was phenomenal—to the point that one night it was taken. The nearby radio, TV, and paper all took the story on, and an extraordinary chase started to locate the sham. I later assessed that this sham and its loss gave my business around $20 000 worth of free publicizing. Before choosing sign-composing, drive around and take a gander at different organizations to perceive what styles you like and what gets your attention. Visit your rivals' workplaces, shops, or on the other hand, production lines to decide how you could make your business signage all the more speaking to potential clients.

Make sure to make your sign-composing match your corporate picture and friends' hues; in any case, things can begin to get untidy and befuddling to your potential clients. Keep all sign-composing straightforward and simple to peruse. The new saying that 'toning it down would be best' unquestionably applies to sign-composing. When you plan your sign-composing, Coincidentally, recollect incorporating what days you are open or exchanging hours. There is nothing more regrettable than sitting outside a business at 8.15 a.m. on a Saturday, pondering if it will open on such day or on the off chance that it will open at 8.30 a.m. or on the other hand 9.00 a.m. Showcasing as the backbone of business How much time do you have to dedicate to advertising?

The more significant part of this book's promoting thoughts will take under 30 minutes to execute. The huge question you have to ask yourself is how much time you would commit to advertising and advancing your business? You might have the option to go through 30 minutes out of each month, or you might be started up and prepared to focus on 30 minutes every day. It doesn't make a difference how much time you dispense as long as you attempt to actualize new thoughts on an ordinary premise. You be the judge on how standard the premise should be.

The time that you commit to promoting your business should be quality time. It is nothing more than trouble attempting to press it in among the thousand and one different obligations that you need to manage every day. I am a firm devotee to promoting endlessly from your business, in a situation where you won't be upset or occupied. In any event, utilize this opportunity to design your procedure and, at that point, do the real executing of thoughts at the workplace.

Numerous business administrators feel that advertising resembles doing bookwork—it is something that you need to do instead of something that you need to do. As a whole, we know what occurs on the off chance that you don't do your book work. Toward the end of the monetary year, you timidly take the shoebox full of receipts to the bookkeeper who gives you 'a look.' You toss the container on the bookkeeper's work area and run out the entryway. A couple of months after the fact, the assessment man rings asking a couple of 'it would be ideal if you clarify' type questions, and in the end, you will have to pay somebody a great deal of cash.

Not doing your showcasing all the time can have an increasingly emotional final product—your business loses everything. The moral is straightforward—you should be taught, and you need to put aside a practical measure of time to showcase your business all the time. How much business do you have to endure? This is the beginning of any promoting effort or plan, and shockingly it is only here and there considered in independent companies. You have to ask yourself the inquiry: how much business do I truly require?

There are two motivations to pose this inquiry. The first is to give you an everyday focus to focus on. If you don't have a clue how much business you need, you will never be fulfilled. The other explanation is to attempt to take out the danger of getting an excessive amount of business—truly, truth is stranger than fiction, a lot of business. The significant activity presently is to take a couple of moments, what's more, turn out precisely how much business you have to cover the entirety of your expenses. Be straightforward and reasonable and overestimate as opposed to thinking little of. You can work out this figure for a year, a month, a week, or a day. I like to work it out on a month-to-month premise, as the greater part of our clients pays once per month.

When you know precisely how much business you need to take care of all costs, you know precisely how much business you need to endure. This is the thing that it will cost you to open the entryways consistently. The subsequent stage is to choose how a lot of benefits you need to make from your business. Add this to your endurance figure and, voila, you currently have a figure to focus on. This discloses to you precisely how much business you need. It is astonishing how clear everything becomes when all of an unexpected, you know how much business you have to endure, and how much business you need to benefit. Very scarcely any organizations set aside the effort to make sense of these objectives. However, effective ones consistently do. The following point, producing an excessive amount of business, brings to mind the accompanying stories. A companion of mine was associated with building an enormous oceanarium. The dispatch of the fascination was extremely large, with many dollars spent on luring swarms for the opening day. Well, the groups came—unmistakably more than the oceanarium had considered—and the outcome was that the day was a debacle. Individuals were stuck in lines for a considerable length of time. The pulverizing of the swarms was insane; the eateries came up short on nourishment, youngsters were lost, individuals swooned, etc.

It required some investment for this appreciation for remaking its notoriety. The terrific opening was a money related achievement yet a total disappointment as far as long haul advertising. The swarms left after a baffling encounter, and thus they advised their loved ones not to trouble to visit the fascination since it was a ruin. Another short story that I have discovered intriguing has to do with smoking. A companion as of late attempted to quit smoking following a serious publicizing effort from the Stop line (several people could call for guidance and backing to stop smoking) on TV. What's more, the realistic blood gore notices were excessively, and the QUIT line appeared to be a spectacular help for anybody attempting to give up the feared nicotine. The promotion worked, and my companion settled on the choice to stop on the spot. Following seven days without cigarettes, she had a snapshot of shortcomings and concluded that she required assistance rapidly—no issues. A quick call to the QUIT line, and everything will be OK. She called the line, was put on hold for ten minutes, and afterward, a somewhat discourteous woman said that she proved unable to help now; however, somebody would get back to soon.

After seven days, somebody called, saying 'sorry' about the delay and fighting that the additional promoting had made them so bustling that they couldn't adapt to the thousands of calls they were getting each day. By this stage, my companion had quit any pretense of attempting to stop her despite everything smokes. There is an important exercise to be scholarly. On the off chance that you begin to do a ton of showcasing, verify that your business can adapt to the expansion. All organizations need the telephone to be running hot, yet few can adapt to an unexpected increment in business without making, at any rate, a couple of operational changes. New clients that go to your business because of your advertising movement will test you to check whether you can convey what you guarantee. On the off chance that you don't dazzle them the first time around, you may never get the chance to attempt again.

For what reason is it critical to appear as something else? Suppose you had a portion of this season's flu virus, and you concluded that you expected to get some medication. Envision you go to the shops and discover ten individual drug stores nearby to each other, all in a pleasant slick line and fundamentally no different. How do you choose which drug store to buy your influenza medicine from? Do you search for the least expensive, the one with the most supportive staff, the greatest, the littlest, the most extended setup, the one you have visited previously, or nearly the nearest? These are the sorts of inquiries that we intuitively ask each time we go to buy a thing. The unavoidable issue is: the thing that makes your business unique from your rivals? If your clients are attempting to pick between your business and your rivals' organizations, why would it be advisable for them to utilize yours? You have to think of the appropriate response to this inquiry, and it should be persuading.

Quite a while back, the celebrated organization Federal Express ended up battling in the profoundly competitive universe of cargo. They concluded that they required an approach or an announcement to clarify why individuals should utilize their great scope of cargo administrations, which were essentially equivalent to each other cargo dispatch in the USA. The promoting organization thought of the trademark, 'If it completely, emphatically must be there medium-term utilise Federal Express.' An enormous battle was propelled to advance this new organisation motto, and the rest is history. Government Express has developed to get one of the most prominent cargo organization on the planet. The fundamental explanation credited to the achievement of this trademark is how it distinguished what makes Government Express not the same as their various rivals by expressing that if it needs to arrive, you would be wise to utilize Federal Express. It infers that if your bundle truly needs to get where it is passing by tomorrow, Federal Express is the main one that can get it there. The absolute best words to utilize when attempting to concoct one straightforward motto that will separate your business from your rivals are the greatest, the biggest, the longest settled, the freshest, the best, the most, ensured, the ideal, the best, the main, the right, the most elevated and the first.

The one thing that is sure in business is that challenge will keep on expanding. There will be more individuals attempting to offer comparative things to a similar number of individuals. Consequently, it is imperative to recognize what makes your business diverse and, eventually, superior to your rivals.

How lot of cash do you have to spend on showcasing? Finding the money to showcase and promote a business is regularly difficult. When challenges are out of hand, individuals will, in general, cut back in the territory of promoting—this is the time that promoting and showcasing ought to be expanded; however, it once in a while happens that way. Most organizations that come to me for guidance have very restricted spending plans—in some cases, as meager as $20 every week. My guidance is consistently the equivalent. The size of the financial backing doesn't matter, yet how you use it does. An organization with a $20 every week advertising spending plan likely needs to create two or three thousand dollars each year. An organization with a million-dollar advertising spending needs to turn more than tens of millions every year.

Deciding how a lot of cash you ought to spend advancing your business is a troublesome choice. The acknowledged approach to land at a showcasing spending plan is a level of your total turnover, somewhere in the range of 5 percent to 20 percent. If the figure you picked was 10 percent and you turn over a million dollars every year, you anticipate spending $100 000 every year in promoting and advertising. It is continuosly insightful to converse with your bookkeeper or monetary counsel regarding setting a financial limit, yet recall, promoting ought to be a fixed cost like lease or power. On the off chance that you don't effectively advance your business, it will vanish before long. On the off chance that you hold up until you are edgy, you are under significantly more strain to get the outcomes. As of late, I had a gem dealer approach me to do a few advertising for his organization. He had been working for over fifteen years, and he had never spent a penny on promoting. This man was effective, yet over the most recent five years, the rivalry had expanded, visitor numbers had dropped furthermore, the business had abruptly got intense. He was modest also; he had done a ton of soul looking to comprehend why his business was fizzling. His most prominent acknowledgment was that he didn't take a functioning position in advertising his business since he imagined that the clients would consistently be there.

Don't feel that you have to have an advertising spending plan for many dollars to produce results. There are a vast number of private ventures that have publicized insightfully for next to no monetary cost. Take a gander at what you can manage the cost of on a week after week premise, put this cash in a safe spot, and evaluate your choices. Do whatever it takes not to be worried about the measure of money that you have accessible—invest the time and vitality choosing how to manage it.

Try not to fear to mention to individuals your financial limit, particularly on the off chance that they are attempting to sell you some promotion. Mention to them what you can bear the cost of and ask them what they can do to advance your business with this measure of cash. Each arrangement is debatable. On the off chance that they need your business seriously enough, they will offer you a motivator to work with them. Another point that merits referencing is that spending any cash on promoting is an exercise in futility on the off chance that you can't give your clients what they need and, all the more critically, what they anticipate. I generally request that business administrators look long and hard at their business before promoting to ensure can meet these desires. After all, what is the purpose of burning through cash on getting new clients to have them gone afterward?

I recall as of late; a themed eatery opened up. They had fabulous pre-opening advertising, and there was an undeniable quality of expectation that the spot was going to be generally excellent. When it, at last, opened, the nourishment was lousy what's more, the theming standard, so individuals didn't return. I anticipate this business to close its entryways sooner rather than later. They sold individuals the guarantee of an enjoyable experience, yet they proved unable to concoct the products. This book recommends many free and minimal effort thoughts that will bring you business. Above all else, ensure that your business can do what you state; it can, at that point, focus on a week after week spending plan to advertise it.

Would you like to discover new clients or continue existing ones?

To put it obtusely, it costs much more to discover new clients than to keep old ones. Figures change from industry to industry, yet it is evaluated that discovering new clients costs nine-fold the number of existing clients. The good to this story is for you to have a decent, legit take a gander at your business and ask yourself the accompanying questions:

1. Do you offer great help and incentive for cash?
2. Do your clients hold returning, or do you see them once and never again?
3. Do you keep in contact with your clients after they have made a buy?
4. Do you reward clients for being faithful to your business?

Lack of concern can be a significant issue, particularly for organizations that have been built up for more than a couple of years. All enterprises are exceptionally serious and never like before, we as a whole should be more brilliant. One of the most astute business systems is to care for your current clients. Support them, urge them to go through additional with your business, persistently approach them for approaches to improve your present administration and scope of items. Keep in contact with your clients, reward them for being steadfast, and they will remain with you for a long time.

The account of a Sydney bistro rings a bell. All regulars at this coffeehouse have their cup. They are quality mugs with the person's name imprinted as an afterthought, and they all hold tight snares on a considerable divider. Regulars stroll into the coffeehouse, snatch their mug, take it to the counter and spot their request—their favored style of the espresso is mechanized and comes up when the client's name is entered. Mug holders are offered an assortment of regular specials. In other words, they are caused to feel exceptionally uncommon. This is a very fruitful bistro — a large number of the thoughts prescribed in this book center around client support. The additional income you're looking for might be nearer than you might suspect.

Do you have 'private company disorder'?

I regularly meet independent company administrators who state that they can't do the kind of advertising that huge enterprises do since they don't have anyplace close to a similar enormous spending plan. I state, why not? I call this the private company disorder, and I hear it frequently.

Large business spends a ton of cash on promoting and promoting. Huge partnerships need to contribute a massive number of dollars to statistical surveying and prominent promoting on TV, radio, and papers to keep up their portion of the market. The rivalry is continuosly solid, and at the day's end, the organizations with the best-promoting, upheld up with great items and generous help, tend to be the best.

How unique is this for an independent venture? I accept that there is no distinction except for the number of zeros connected to the spending limit's size. On the off chance that a publicizing or advertising thought works for an enormous organization, for what reason wouldn't you be able to, the independent company administrator, receive a similar thought?

A prime case of this is the client reliability program utilized by numerous huge organizations. The most outstanding devotion programs are the long-standing customer battles offered by, for all intents and purposes, each carrier around the globe. This framework's fundamental standard is that the more you fly with one specific organization (and its related accomplice aircraft), the more free flights and different rewards you will get. For what reason can't any independent company utilize this guideline from a coffeehouse to a vehicle wash? Prize your clients for being faithful. By doing this, you recognize that your clients have a decision, and they have picked you.

The dedication program is discussed in more detail later in this book. There are numerous different thoughts utilized by an enormous business that can, without much of a stretch, be adjusted and used by littler organizations for a small amount of the expense. Disregard the 'independent venture disorder' and utilize the thoughts that huge partnerships have demonstrated to work; at that point, harvest the awards of their speculation. Significant companies use the entirety of the ideas in this book.

What is statistical surveying, and do you need it?

A great many people in business either disregard statistical surveying as something that lone huge organizations can manage the cost of or, on the other hand, they class it as one of those terms that individuals toss around without truly understanding what it implies. Statistical surveying is one of the most dominant advertising apparatuses for any business. Statistical surveying is essentially inquiring about potential clients or existing clients (here and there) a couple of necessary inquiries. The responses to these inquiries are then used to detail the eventual fate of your business.

Statistical surveying is significantly less expensive than going belly up because of a terrible choice. For instance, envision that you run a bread shop, and you are contemplating adding a takeaway nourishment outlet to the front of the industrial facility. There are two different ways that you can go about this. The first is to purchase the entirety of the new hardware, utilize the staff, change the signage, promote and afterward sit back and trust that the group separates the entryway. This is how most of the business thoughts will, in general advance; also, for each one that works, hundreds come up short.

The subsequent approach to this task is to do a piece of statistical surveying first. Plan a couple of necessary inquiries to ask your clients. For instance:

1. Do you purchase lunch from a takeaway eatery?
2. How far do you need to travel?

3. Is the nourishment acceptable, or do you shop there because it is helpful?
4. On the off chance that we had a takeaway nourishment outlet, would you consider attempting us?
5. What sort of nourishment might you want to have the option to purchase for lunch?
6. What different things do you need all the time that you figure we should stock (for instance, papers, magazines, and so forth.)?
7. Would it be helpful for you on the off chance that we were open late toward the evening so you could buy pre-made suppers to bring home for supper?
8. The subsequent stage is to begin conversing with everybody who could be a potential client. Pay somebody to go entryway to-entryway or hop on the telephone and start ringing potential clients. Many people are happy to answer an overview as long as you rapidly explain your identity and what you need and underscore that it will just take a couple of moments.

What promotional material are you using?

Extraordinary material advances as your business develop. Today it might be a straightforward, one-page, photocopied flyer that can be dropped into letterboxes if that is all that you can bear. Maybe tomorrow you will have a gleaming magazine including your workplaces around the globe. The primary point is to consistently make the best limited-time material that you can manage the cost of at the time. Individuals will size up your organization depends on your limited time material. Fruitful organizations have excellent quality, a unique material that they are glad to pass out. Special material spreads everything from business cards to handouts, flyers, signage, outfits, and sites. The most well-known advertising shortcoming I have watched is that independent companies, for the most part, have inferior limited time material. Leaflets are jumbled with masses of data, poor shading decisions, and a total need for energy. They are difficult to peruse, and they are exhausting. It doesn't make a difference what your item is; more individuals will use it if it looks intriguing and energizing and your organization looks proficient and secure.

There is a confusion that to deliver conspicuous handouts costs a ton of cash—it used to. Today there is a part of innovation around that has made creating unique material significantly less expensive. On the off chance that you don't have the foggiest idea what you need, attempt to discover tests of unique material that you like and duplicate the configuration or the format (be careful with copyright laws that make it unlawful to duplicate things precisely). Take the test to a creator or work area distributor and get them to style your limited time material around the example you have given. Toward the day's end, it costs a similar measure of cash to deliver a lousy leaflet as it does to create a decent one. Take the time, get the exhortation, and make your limited time material the best quality that you can bear.

Be glad to show individuals your flyers, business cards, and leaflets. Another point to recollect is the familiar axiom that a picture is better than a thousand words when selling items. Continuously utilize photos where conceivable furthermore, attempt to make the images the best quality accessible. It truly is generally economical to have pictures taken in a studio, and the outcomes are fantastic. These photos imitated in your limited time material will look a thousand times superior to the glad snap of you at the seashore. From my experience, excellent limited time material outcomes in great deals. If you have poor limited time material, be sufficiently large to change. I have seen numerous organizations that barely care about burning through $200 000 to set up their business; however, they recoil at burning through $2000 to deliver a quality pamphlet.

Another significant point to recollect with limited time material is to make it stand apart from the group and your restriction. Continuously analyze pamphlets, search for new, inventive thoughts that grab your eye, and most significantly, distinguish what makes you need to purchase a specific item. If it chipped away at you, maybe it will work for your potential clients.

Do you need a holiday to get started?

Are you feeling dynamic and prepared to jump into showcasing, or then again, is this the final desperate attempt at endurance? Many little business administrators come to me at the distress arrange, totally worn out with their nerves tense. My showcasing guidance to them is to have an occasion. An uplifting frame of mind is the best weapon that any business proprietor or supervisor can have. Now and then, it is simpler said than done. Be that as it may, from my experience, there are two unmistakable sorts of businessmen. The main type opens the entryways and trusts that the clients will begin coming in. They, for the most part, try not to promote, saying that it is an exercise in futility and cash. The clients don't get through the entryway, so they start to get disappointed, and they become increasingly negative as every day passes by. There are a hundred reasons why the business isn't working, and nothing is their deficiency—it's the economy or the person up the street or the administration.

From my experience, these organizations become penniless—regularly. Positive and bright individuals control the second sort of business. They are attractive, well disposed, and open to thoughts. They have confidence in attempting various ways to deal with promoting and publicizing. They comprehend that promoting is a fundamental piece of their business. Their clients leave this business happy with their experience, and, taking all things together probability, they will return and tell loads of others about their experience. These organizations will, in general, succeed.

It isn't really how much cash you have in the bank or how much experience you have that decides the achievement of your business. An inspirational frame of mind and eagerness for doing are two advantageous assets in the effective specialist's ordnance. On the off chance that you are roasted, how might you hope to get excellent outcomes from promoting? It is never a decent time to have an occasion—possibly you are excessively occupied, or you haven't got any cash, or there is nobody to take care of the business when you are away.

A companion of mine runs an electrical machine fix shop. This is a requesting business that consistently requires him to be shouted to fix machines. He frequently whined about how caught he felt in his business. An opportunity introduced itself for him to go to Antarctica for ten weeks. As he was an eager picture taker, the chance was too acceptable to even think about passing up, yet he was profoundly worried that his clients wouldn't comprehend and he would lose his business. He went in any case, essentially closing the business for the time he was no more. To put it plainly, he had the excursion of a lifetime, and, half a month after showing up home, it was nothing new. He may have lost a couple of clients; however, he has gotten new ones generally rapidly. The occasion did him a ton of good and more than likely did his business a lot of good since he returned revived and positive. The good of this story is that there will never be a great time to have a break, yet now and then, you shouldn't let that stop you.

Identify your competitors

It is fundamentally imperative to know precisely what items and administrations your rivals offer. How might you contend against a business if you don't know what you are going up against? From my involvement in a private venture, when you get some information about contending organizations, there are two general reactions. The first is that they start a searing discourse on how clumsy their rivals are, the ticket costly, how problematic, etc. The subsequent reaction is an astonishing look mirroring the way that they know nothing about their opponents.

A significant principle in maintaining an effective business is to verify that you and your staff never thump a contender under any circumstance. On the off chance that you are dubious about the work that they give, say as much; however, never criticize them or their items. Figure out how to sell your business on your characteristics, not the restriction's deficits. To discover data about your rivals is very simple. You can call the organization legitimately, read through their notices, ask your loved ones if they have utilized this business, and ask them how they discovered the administration that they got. When you are sure about what they offer, you can advance your business around what makes you unique and ideally better, with the goal that potential clients will purchase from you. Numerous organizations see contenders as the foe when in all actuality, they can be companions. Keen organizations working together can frame extremely solid collusion. For instance, envision two cleaning organizations helping one another and cooperating. Envision for a second that these two organizations conclude that if either is too occupied to even think about doing something when a client calls, they will prescribe the other.

If one forces short on cleaning synthetic compounds to leave hours, the other will assist. They can concede to the limits and the customers that each organization will target (be cautious about estimating illicit to fix costs in numerous nations). If you are sufficiently fortunate to have the option to work with your rivalry, that is incredible. If not, in any event, come to a meaningful conclusion of knowing and understanding what the challenge offers with the goal that you can provide more.

Dr. T. Anderson

Have you had terrible encounters with advertising before?

I frequently hear business administrators saying that they attempted this, or on the other hand, they attempted that, and it didn't work. They, at that point, make excellent articulations. For example, TV publicizing is a waste of cash, or paper publicising doesn't work. I attempt to recommend that many elements that make showcasing work, and you have to have the same number of them on your side as conceivable to get results. I recall quite a while before a companion who runs a noticeable vacation spot ran a Mother's Day extraordinary offer in the paper. The notice said that all moms could have free confirmation on Mother's Day. The paper committed an error and multiplied the size of the notice. The outcome was astounding, and the fascination had their busiest day on record. The next year they reran a similar ad at the more prominent size, reasoning that it was the size of the ad that had delivered these stunning outcomes. This time they had a spectacular day. Why? On the past Mother's Day, it was pouring with downpour what's more; this fascination was covert. The climate on the most recent Mother's Day was electrifying, so everybody was outside. Add to this an immense celebration that circumstantially ran around the same time, and what was an effective advancement the year before transformed into a catastrophe the year after. I am attempting to make sure that conventional promoting mediums, like TV, radio, and paper, work. If none of them isn't working, all you need to do is evacuate what didn't work and attempt it once more. When you hit the nail on the head, don't change the recipe until it quits working.

Another intriguing point that I have watched is that individuals' desires for the business they will produce from promoting is frequently unreasonable. I meet individuals who think that a $50 commercial will acquire $50 000. On the off chance that it did, each business would be sufficient. The truth of the matter is that there are no enchantment equations to reveal how much business you ought to expect when you place a promotion. If you can spread the ad's expense, you are in front—everything else is a reward. Fruitful advertising involves diligence to get the recipe right.

Transform your receipt into a business instrument

Most organizations convey solicitations and explanations on a standard premise. Solicitations are regularly gone through several hands before they contact the individual that signs the check. This gives you a chance to elevate your business to various individuals who are effectively mindful of what you essentially do; however, maybe not of each aspect of your business brings to the table. This is the thing that we call a 'delicate sell' or 'encouraging feedback' of your organization's message. Maybe you will stock another range or item, perhaps evaluating has changed, or then again, your exchanging hours are unique, or you need to strengthen the solid corporate message you are now putting over.

A PC programming organization I managed utilized their organization receipt to present another individual from staff each month. For instance, January's receipt had an image of Bill Higgins, Sales Manager, with a straightforward layout of his professional history and what job he played in the organization.

This gave a unique vibe to their business and expanded my level of mindfulness regarding the individuals I was managing. The presentation of an organization staff part likewise took the accentuation of the receipt is a bill. I am sure that I paid these records a lot snappier because they had a very individual feel. I also felt as though I was a piece of that organization, an esteemed client being demonstrated an effective business's internal operations. Another organization that I used to manage sent continuously out a flyer with jokes, positive certifications, persuasive sections, and extensive, fascinating material. It was always a happiness to get these solicitations, and I realize that these were paid early. They put a grin all over, so I accepted that they had the right to be paid rapidly. What number of bills do you anticipate accepting?

I have likewise known about this strategy being utilized when individuals are late paying their solicitations. Put an image of your family in the envelope with a quick note on the back saying that it is 'difficult to nourish our youngsters when your organisation is slow taking care of their tab.' This is extremely powerful. You may need to pick your client as this may not be suitable for a few. This thought can be made very clever relying upon how you do it, maybe sending a photo of your pooch taking a gander at an empty supper bowl or a vacant treat container or something comparable. Another viable method to get individuals to see and peruse your solicitations is to utilize extremely brilliant hues. Our solicitations are sent on fluorescent green paper that nearly shines in obscurity. It is continuously an icebreaker on the off chance that we are pursuing a past due record as everybody recollects the notorious lime green receipt.

Solicitations can turn out to be excellent, showcasing devices, and, remarkably, the most terrible that can happen is that you get paid quicker. As you are, as of now conveying solicitations, the main additional expense is in the flyer's generation.

Sell yourself in any event, when you're not there

Everyone detests being put on hold; however, tragically, it is a lifestyle. On the off chance that you have the innovation to play hold music, you can most likely mastermind to have an organization message playing. This is a fortunate time to tell potential clients increasingly about your organzation and the administrations that you offer.

Many organizations mastermind 'messages on hold,' and the expense isn't excessively costly. As the more significant part of these advertising thoughts, it is increasingly only somebody making an opportunity to discover the organization that produces 'messages on hold' and afterward really orchestrating the administration to be introduced. This sort of advertising produces a very great corporate picture, and numerous little organizations give the appearance of being a massive organization by having expert on-hold messages. A similar standard can apply with replying to mail furthermore, voice messages on cell phones.

Utilize the Internet for publicity

The Internet is another and energizing asset that has immense potential. Promoting on the Internet is another idea that numerous oragnizations don't generally comprehend. I, for one, take a gander at the Internet as an important library. You know that the entirety of the data is there; it's merely a question of discovering it. The measure of data accessible is unbelievable; however, the way to progress is by making it simple for individuals to discover your business or item. Fundamentally there are two different ways to advance your business on the Internet. The first is that you can have your site where individuals surfing the net may run over your site and conclude that they need more data or that they might want to buy what you are selling. Setting up your site is turning out to be less expensive consistently, and inside several years, most of the organizations will have their claim sites. Sites can undoubtedly be connected to different locales, making it more straightforward for you to be found.

There are organizations accessible that sell completely structured what's more, extremely great sites that you buy. They fill in the spaces and put your organization name and your items and administrations in a suitable spot. So for a couple of hundred dollars, you can have an exceptionally proficient site ready for action. To discover these organizations scan for 'site facilitating, website architecture and area names' on the Internet. A significant number of organizations that offer this administration publicize vigorously on web search tool destinations. The following method to advance your business on the Web is to buy what is known as standard notices. This is the place you put a notice on another person's site. The benefit of this is that you can advance your business on a profoundly fruitful site set up and maybe get a vast number of 'hits' every month. To underscore this point, envision you have composed a book on Alien Abductions, and you have concluded that the Web is the medium to advance and sell the book. For around 300 dollars, you could set up a site with a fundamental design and kick back and trust who individuals discover you. The option is to put in two or three thousand dollars and take a flag commercial at a setup UFO site— one that has up to 70 000 'hits' or visits every day. The ad will cost a great deal of cash; however, you approach countless individuals that have just demonstrated an enthusiasm for the subject you have expounded on. The Internet is an excellent instrument with boundless potential. While I had a brisk swim on the Internet as of late, I ran over foods grown from the ground store that home conveys their produce all through the city. You email them your request, and it is conveyed that day. They have a virtual supermarket on the Net, and you essentially glance through the products and make your buys by Visa.

I was at a class as of late when the host clarified how his American-based oragnization obtained their letterhead and business cards from a printer in Malaysia using the Internet. They used to purchase their stationery from the printer nearby to them; however, they found that the products they requested from Malaysia showed up faster and were less costly. Presently the challenge isn't the shop up the street yet the entirety of the shops far and wide. Try not to be frightened of the Web—use it to further your potential benefit. Make sure to incorporate your email address or site on the entirety of your particular material and in any ad.

Dr. T. Anderson

Benefit as much as possible from packaging

Numerous organizations give packaging to their items. This might be something as straightforward as a modest plastic pack right through to a substantial wooden container. Bundling gives the ideal open door for an organization message to be passed on to potential clients that see the bundling just as the client gets the bundle. If you are giving the bundling, why not utilize it to expand your deals. Print an organization motto on your wrapping paper, maybe your exchanging hours, blessing proposals, new items, change of address data, or whatever other messages that you can consider.

Another simple thought that is once in a while utilized is to slip in a limited time flyer when bundling up a thing. On the off chance that an individual has purchased something from your business, there is a decent chance that they will buy something different later on or maybe prescribe you to a companion. Book shops are one of only a handful, not many enterprises, that genuinely exploit the capability of in-bundling advancements. Most will incorporate a flyer covering specials of the month, most recent discharges, and exceptional intrigue type distributions, too, as giving you a free bookmark advancing a most recent discharge. I caught wind of a thought in Japan where a significant shopping focus in Tokyo has a city map imprinted on their packs. Individuals all over town go around finding their way through the rushing about with this itemized guide, which also advances the inside as the best spot to shop in Tokyo.

Keep in mind the significance of a business card.

Business cards are often seen as a vital insidiousness rather than an extraordinary showcasing instrument. Potential clients conclude a great deal from your appearance and that of your business card. Put forth the attempt and utilise your business card to its full potential. Business cards are ordinarily imprinted in sheets, which implies that you can have various messages or then again names. By all methods, utilize some for names; however, use the others as smaller than usual pamphlets. Putting your administrations on the back of a business card adds barely to the creation cost; however, it upgrades your card, and makes it a powerful device.

Another choice is to have 'get this card and get the accompanying... ' on your business card. Bistros appear to have received this thought on mass with for all intents and purposes each bistro offering an espresso card where you pay for such a significant number of cups also; you get one free. The business card is your advancement record, which is checked off each time you make a buy. This idea functions admirably with eateries that offer either a free glass of wine or a free sweet with supper. The offer is imprinted on the rear of the card, and to recover it, the client must deliver the card when feasting.

Numerous oragnizations could utilize this idea to effectively build the business they accept from new and existing clients. When you have ultimately used your business cards, the following significant advance is to disseminate them all over. The cost distinction between printing 2000 and 3000 business cards is, indeed, very little—the more you print, the less expensive they become. Put them on noticeboards, in letterboxes, remain on your counter, offer them to your providers, mail them out, or stay on a traffic intersection giving them out.

Individuals spare business cards. If yours looks excellent and has more data about your oragnization than only the business name, you can wager that individuals will cling to it. One approach to urge individuals to cling to your business card is to make it a telephone card. Organizations that practice making telephone cards are regularly more than ready to arrange where you purchase a specific number of telephone cards from them, and they will print your organization message on the front. They may considerably offer a couple of dollars in free calls with the expectation that the individual getting the card will energize it once the underlying credit is utilized. Any irregular business card thoughts will, for the most part, be acceptable for standing out. I have seen some incredible melodic business cards, scented business cards, and even gleam in the dim business cards. Take a gander at printing business cards as an opportunity, not as an errand. Have a ton of fun and attempt to think of an abnormal thought that will cause individuals to sit up; what's more, pay heed to your business basically because you have built up an irregular business card.

It is less expensive to continue existing clients than it is to discover new ones. Fruitful organizations take a stab at building strong associations with their clients. They reward them for shopping typically; they request input, they search for approaches to continually improve both the items and the administrations they are advertising. They likewise never underestimate their clients. The ideal way to care for existing clients is to keep in contact with them. If you haven't done this before, don't stress, it is never too late to send somebody a letter that appreciates them for being a customer. The thoughts we'll discuss in this segment are:

1. Send out update takes note
2. Stay in contact with your clients
3. Remember significant dates
4. Ask your clients for referrals
5. Say thank you so you can increase your business transactions
6. What is a steadfastness program, and would you be able to utilize one?

Keep in contact with your clients

I was, as of late, drew nearer by a little aluminum fabricating organization. They made some troublesome memories as their specific industry had gotten serious in the most recent couple of years. Following a couple of moments of talking about what the principle issue was (insufficient clients), I asked how they had been doing business since quite a while ago. My jaw dropped when they said just about twenty years, and during that time, they had only about 20 000 clients.

In the wake of examining for a couple of more subtleties, it got apparent that once a vocation was done and conveyed, this business had no further contact with the client. There was no follow-up or after-deals administration. Sitting on the floor in some dusty corner was a case loaded up with the names of thousands of clients that had just utilized this business; however, they had never been followed up. This is a typical shortcoming of little business administrators. They don't keep in contact with their past clients since they don't have the foggiest idea what to state. The primary item that the organization offered was the selling and establishment of carport entryways. It showed up coherent that they should offer a free after-deals administration call where they visit the house to oil the entryway, pressure the chain also, for the most part, ensure that everything is functioning admirably. This gives two chances. In the first place, the client feels great because the degree of administration they have gotten is incredible; also, they will tell their companions. The subsequent open door is that the administration individual speaking to the oraganization can coolly different layout administrations and items accessible, ideally making another deal.

If you have boxes of past customer records lying in a dusty corner, uncover them and find a good pace, first of all, beginning correspondence with them. Drop them a line and ask how your item is holding up. Tell them that you will send refreshes about new and enegizing items and administrations later on. These individuals have, as of now, strolled through your entryway once. Accepting they were upbeat with your business, what is going to prevent them from returning once more? Arrange the records, check the addresses, telephone numbers, and so forth, and ensure that they are state-of-the-art and afterward begin. Your best wellspring of business could be concealed in the nursery shed under a pile of National Geographic magazines and old assessment records.

Approach your clients for referrals

Referrals are basically when you approach a current client for the name of somebody they realize might have the option to utilize your administrations or items. The primary thought is that you contact the individual being alluded and let them know that your client prescribed that you call them. It is equivalent to having somebody within. By referencing the companion's or client's name as a proposal, you consequently have your foot in the entryway. Referrals are an extraordinary method to produce new business. Setting up a framework where your present customers can furnish you with the name of a companion or associate who might be keen on your item or administration is a very cheap approach to create additional business. It is smart to offer some remuneration for clients who offer referrals, for example, a free item or free assistance. Numerous quality organizations get an enormous extent of their business from client referrals. Significantly, you feel sufficiently sure to approach your clients for referrals—if they are content with the work you have done, is there any valid reason why they wouldn't be glad to give a lead to another client? You might be astounded at how willing individuals are to assist you with advancing your business. As an ordinary business practice, it is smart to communicate to the client after all work is finished to make certain that they are 100 percent fulfilled. This is the ideal time to request the referral and to verify indeed that they are content with the work that you have done.

Dr. T. Anderson

Continuously be forthcoming and genuine.

I have regularly told my clients when I am experiencing a calm time, and I need some more work. Out of nowhere, I have a group of agents pursuing a business for me. I generally locate this very lowering and ring to state thank you for their assistance. There are many sceptical individuals on the planet; however, I do accept that most of the individuals will make a special effort to help others. As an end-result of this, I will consistently give 100 percent to individuals who helped me before. Try not to be hesitant to request that your clients propose a few referrals for your business.

Get behind a wacky advancement.

Probably the best thought I have found out about as of late was a rancher in England who sold promoting on his bovines. A neighborhood frozen yogurt organization moved toward the rancher. They made up cover like standards for the cows to wear highlighting the message: 'Our fundamental fixing originates from here' (or then again something like this). The ranch was situated alongside probably the busiest roadways, which implied that tens of thousands of individuals saw these 'dairy animals with signs' each day. That was the little part. The promoting bovines were so unordinary they were highlighted on TV around the globe. The dessert organization got an inconceivable presentation, and the expense of the advancement was negligible when you consider the intrigue is created. This is an exceptionally astute thought with heaps of utilisations to anybody in the business. From time to time, you might be drawn nearer to engage in some unusual advancement, for example, a kissing rivalry. We regularly compose these thoughts off as being excessively a long way from planet earth—well, speculation once more. Two hundred fifty million individuals around the globe see insane games like Extreme Games. Individuals love insane— the top-rating TV programs incorporate Funniest Home Recordings, Cops, The World's Craziest People, and Ripley's Believe It Or Not.

More often than not, when individuals approach you about engaging in advancements like this, they are after gifts of items or time. Try not to discount these thoughts. Get behind them and ensure that your organization's name is everywhere throughout the advancement. Why not be the one to concoct the idea? Ensure it is possible and attempt to get a couple of individuals associated with the arranging stages to ensure you keep your feet on the ground. The most terrible that can happen is that you have a great deal of fun.

Utilize inflatable toys to boost your business

This type of promotion is developing in fame, particularly in the last few years, as rivalry for outside signage increments. No uncertainty having a colossal explode dinosaur or comedian or inflatable on your rooftop will stand out. These curiosities can be contracted, once again moderately reasonably, in most capital urban communities. They can be utilized for a grand opening, during a deal, or for any other festival where you need to grab individuals' eye. They can be mighty if your business is situated on a significant street. When you understand how a lot of cash can be spent on promoting a deal, the oddity thought like the airship can be a very savvy expansion to your advertising effort.

Banners are likewise well known as they empower a lively vibe to any occasion and can be seen from a serious separation away. Explode strongholds are another phenomenal plan to help fabricate the climate, and they likewise keep the children involved while Mum and Dad go out on the town to shop. Tragically a few inflatables and inflatable characters have been utilized a great deal, and they begin to look worn, filthy, what's more, decrepit. Before submitting, attempt to see the inflatable gadget set up to verify that all is OK. Another point to mind is neighborhood government guidelines. Ensure you are permitted to have an inflatable toy in plain view. The best spot to discover these kinds of curious things is in the Yellow Pages under 'Advancements,' or if you are out, what's more, you see an inflatable item that you like, the number will presumably be imprinted on it someplace. On the off chance that most noticeably awful comes to most noticeably awful, I would prescribe strolling into the shop being advanced and ask them where the inflatable is employed.

Offer competition prizes

Foundations and donning clubs are continually searching for organizations to give prizes as sponsorship. Organizations that provide products or administrations are, for the most part, offered introduction as exposure, for example, logos on unique material. At the point when these solicitations land on the fax or via telephone, the more significant part of us will, in general, arrange them as a minor bothering rather than a showcasing opportunity. The time has come to retrain those musings.

The individual looking for sponsorship is after an administration or item that your organization sells by and large. By giving this, you are parting with something with retail esteem that you follow through on the cost for. For whatever length of time, the association can offer you a great introduction (recorded as a hard copy), this is a decent bargain. As usual, the greater exposure the challenge or occasion is promising, the better worth you get for your promoting dollar. Frequently prizes that you give additionally charge deductible as a promoting cost. Whenever somebody calls you requesting a prize or sponsorship, ask yourself the accompanying inquiries:

- What is the actual expense of the award that you will be giving?
- What exposure will you get for taking an interest?
- What will individuals see in your organization's name (around)?
- Can you contact these numerous individuals for the expense of the prize with customary publicizing?

More often than not, you will see that these sorts of sponsorships arrive at many individuals; they make your business seem a piece of the neighborhood network (which it ought to be); what's more, they return great introduction for a minimal cost. Individuals love to win things. The vast majority of us seldom win; however, at the point when we do, it's a great deal of fun. We live with the expectation of winning; consequently, we purchase lottery tickets, bet at gambling clubs, punt at the races, and, for the most part, live in anticipation of winning the large one.

Take a stab at plunking down and assembling a challenge to urge individuals to utilize your business. There are a couple of rules to consider before setting out on this undertaking:

- ✓ Check on gaming guidelines to ensure that you can run a challenge in your general vicinity.
- ✓ Make the prize something that you would need to win.
- ✓ Make it simple for individuals to enter.
- ✓ Let individuals enter the same number of times as they need to.
- ✓ Make sure that you advance the challenge.

Rivalries don't bring to the table enormous prizes, be that as it may, there should be prizes that individuals might want to win. A companion of mine possesses a nation lodging. Consistently she parts with a container of brew and a meat plate in a pool that is allowed to enter. This advancement costs her about $50 every week. One of the states of winning is that you must be at the lodging when the prize is drawn someplace between 5 p.m. and 7 p.m. on Friday. As you can envision, the bar is packed, and the draw is a significant piece of the night.

There is nothing to stop you from parting with a prize each week, and somehow or another bunches of little prizes can be better than one major one as you will wind up with progressively glad victors. Regularly backers can be discovered who supply the prizes gratis as a byproduct of the exposure.

Another special reward of having a challenge where individuals leave their name, phone number, and mailing address are that you presently have a mailing list that can be utilized in direct showcasing efforts. I have never been to a specialist's medical procedure. They offer free counsel as a prize or a specialist where one fortunate client for each week wins a vehicle enumerating or free assistance and adjustment. Be creative and recollect that each individual who enters the challenge is a potential client.

Contemplate advertising your business

Perhaps the best recommendation I have ever been given (furthermore, passed on) is to look outside your industry for promoting thoughts. This may not seem like a lot of promoting a thought, yet trust me, it is. If you go throughout the day concentrating on what you do and what your rivals do, what's more, what your clients do, you can turn out to be exceptionally isolated. The final product of this is all organizations inside a specific industry begin to appear to be identical. For instance, examine a couple of dental, medical procedures. They are all precisely the equivalent. Vehicle rental workplaces all seem to be identical. Legal counselors' workplaces, specialists, scientific experts, butchers, bread cooks, and candle creators begin to appear identical. Is there anything incorrectly with this? Not so much.

Notwithstanding, on the off chance that you look outside of your specific industry, you may find a universe of promoting thoughts that would work superbly for your business. I encountered this direct when I had a SCUBA diving shop numerous years prior. At the time, there was a pattern for jump shops to be completely brimming with gear, with a fish tank, an old angling net on the divider with the obligatory plastic fish and crabs, and a couple of geniunely cool-looking fellows running the spot with studs and pigtails. My business was battling. I was youthful with positively no thought of running my own life, not to mention business. To stop a long story, I was edgy. One day a man pulled up before the store in a red Porsche. He came inside and presented himself, saying that a companion of mine prescribed that he visit me. He offered to turn my business around for a level expense of $8000 (at the time, I would have been fortunate to have five dollars). I graciously expressed profound gratitude; however, not this time. The months moved by, and business was going from awful to more terrible. In an odd new development, I joined a lotto syndicate promoted in the paper, and I won $8000. As opposed to taking care of a couple of tabs, I called the person who had visited me and said that I needed his assistance as quickly as could be expected under the circumstances. After I paid him (money in advance, I might include), I began to have profound reservations. My freshly discovered friend in need went to the shop and spent barely any days sticking around and recording things irately. He didn't let out the slightest peep; he watched. After seven days, he gave me a short report with a couple of pages of recommendations for what I ought to do to turn my business around. As I read through his suggestions, my heart sank. His thoughts and suggestions were insane, and I thought I was no more.

A couple of months after the fact, I was indeed nearly shutting down. I pulled out the report that I had been given prior and read through the suggestions. The fundamental ones are recorded underneath:

- split the measure of stock that we convey;
- twofold the cost of everything;
- paint the shop sky blue and hang craftsmanship from the dividers;
- present a 100 percent unconditional promise on everything;
- dispose of the pigtails and hoops and put all staff in formal attire;
- begin selling jump gear on the fund;
- offer the most flawlessly tremendous help for all that we do; and
- offer SCUBA tank tops off for nothing out of pocket.

By this stage, I had nothing left to lose, so I did everything on his rundown. Fundamentally I diverted the store from a jump shop into a 'plunge boutique.' Our turnover significantly increased in the main month. The change was meaningful, and I learned presumably the most critical exercise in my business life—the capacity to look from the outside in at your business or from the back to front (like a goldfish). Lamentably I had association issues a couple of months afterward, and the company wound up shutting in any case. Yet, I knew that it had been convoluted on the off chance that solitary I had made the changes a half year sooner (or maybe not had accomplices).

For what reason did my business consultant's abnormal proposals work? Since he took a gander at the jump shop as a business, not as a jump shop. The proposals he made were to fix up a weak retail business, not a debilitated jump shop. To put it plainly, he utilized his experience from every other industry to offer solutions to fix mine. As a showcasing specialist, I generally think that it's simple to offer guidance for weak organizations because their issues are so obvious to me. For the individuals that possess these organizations, their days are spent adjusting staff, clients, bank accounts, the children, and everything else. It is exceptionally troublesome to have the option to take a gander at what you are doing when you are in this franticness.

Consequently, it is now and again simpler to take a gander at different organizations outside your industry to perceive what they are doing and, in particular, what they are progressing admirably. Search for thoughts that you can utilize and afterward adjust them to suit your business, paying little heed to regardless of whether it is the business-standard. These thoughts are not limited to promoting thoughts, and they spread anything from how you pick up the telephone to how you serve clients.

Incidentally, I never observed Mr. Red Porsche again, and I never had the chance to express gratitude toward him. On the off chance that by some possibility, he is perusing, this I trust it carries a grin to his face.

5
BUILDING BUSINESS CREDIT

What's the ideal approach to begin building business credit quickly? If you need to start promptly and construct your business acknowledge at the earliest opportunity, this post is for you. We will cover demonstrated approaches to building up credit in your organization's name while simultaneously securing your credit. Along these lines, regardless of whether you need access to working capital, acknowledge charge card installments, moderate money Þow or oversee fuel costs, you can begin building business acknowledgment quick for each one of these. To start with, before you make a move, you will need to set up a separate legitimate element for your business. Also, acquire a business identification number (EIN), which isn't utilized for the charge.

It's likewise critical that your organization is 'credit prepared,' implying that it satisfies the guideline prerequisites that banks, loan specialists, providers, retailers, and merchants use as a feature of their credit necessary leadership process. We shall consider several approaches to building business credit.

Approach 1: 'How to Build Business Credit Step by Step.'

Here are five different ways to begin building business credit quick:

1) Switch to Processing Fee Reporting – If you acknowledge Mastercard installments from clients, then why not change to a dealer processor that assembles your business credit? With handling expenses revealing your business can construct its credit profile each time it acknowledges a client's Mastercard instalment.

Handling expenses are expenses that a dealer account supplier charges for their administrations. Commonly, these expenses are a level of each Mastercard exchange in addition to a for each exchange charge for specific kinds of charges.

What's imperative to acknowledge is on the off chance that you acknowledge charge card installments from clients you as of now pay preparing expenses to your vendor account supplier. You don't benefit from your convenient installments to the processor answering your organization's business credit profile. By changing to a shipper supplier that has preparing expense, revealing you beneýt from something, your business is doing. Snap HERE for more subtleties on the most proficient method to get handling charge detailing.

2) Get Business Credit Building Cards – Be sure to look at an ongoing post where we secured the '5 Key Factors to Know Before You Get a Business Credit Card'. The main factor we talked about isn't all business charge cards to construct your business credit. Presently there are card guarantors, such as American Express, that report installment action to both customer and business credit offices, yet despite everything impacting your credit.

On the off chance that you will probably assemble business acknowledge as quickly as conceivable, you can get 4-5 business Mastercards that lone report to the business credit announcing organizations through our UBF financing program. The subsidizing procedure takes 14-20 days, with each card being given in your organization's name. This will empower you to set up 4-5 positive records just answering your organization's credit proýle not close to home credit. Therefore, your business will have its credit character and business FICO assessment fabricated.

3) Utilize Vendor Lines of Credit – With a seller credit extension, you can buy items or administrations for your business with net 30-day terms. These assists preserve with liquidating þow also set up a positive exchange reference for the business. Merchant credit is by a long shot probably the simplest type of business credit to get since the dominant part of merchants don't require an individual credit check and have

insignificant prerequisites for endorsement. Even though you have more than 500,000 sellers, the nation over ready to stretch out credit terms to organizations like yours; not all report installment action to business credit detailing offices. In reality, under 6,000 share installment information with a business credit office. In this way, on the off chance that you need to fabricate business credit quickly, you should choose merchants that report to business acknowledge organizations, for example, Dun and Bradstreet, Experian Business, or Equifax Small Business. For more subtleties and sources, make sure to look at our post on net 30 organizations that report to the business credit revealing organizations. For a total rundown of sellers that report, look at our business credit building framework.

4) Acquire Retail Business Card Accounts – Major retailers, for example, Best Buy, Staples, Home Terminal, Lowes, Costco, and Sears, to give some examples oüer business card records to little organizations. Retail business card accounts work like a customary charge card, with the fundamental diüerence being that it tends to be utilized distinctly at the giving retailer.

The uplifting news is business card accounts are simpler to meet all requirements for contrasted with business credit cards and may accompany different benefits; for example, limits or of buys from the retailer. You might need to be cautious because the loan fees are higher, so it's ideal to pay your balance in full to keep away from intrigue charges. Remember to fit the bill for business accounts with significant retailers. Notably, your business, as of now, has its credit proýle and scores set up. Most of all, major retailers require a few exchange references on their business credit applications and will check your organization's acknowledgment as a component of their credit necessary leadership process. The uplifting news is our bit by bit business credit building framework is intended to move you through each period of the credit building process so your organization can fit the bill for merchant credit, retail-based credit, business charge cards, and different types of financing.

5) Obtain a Company Fleet Card or Gas Card – A fleet card is a fuel card to support a business deal with its costs related to all the organization's vehicles. For the most part, it's utilized by organizations for the following fuel, fix, and upkeep of at least two organization vehicles. An independent company gas card is better used for a business with a solitary vehicle. Albeit both sorts of records have comparative uses, the þeet card is a superior alternative for a business with high gas utilization since there are more prominent cost investment funds related to fleet cards.

The two kinds of cards help fabricate business credit since they report to business credit revealing organizations. By utilizing a fleet or gas card for your organization's fuel costs, you set up progressing credit and installment movement on your organization's credit. Remember, to meet all requirements for a þeet or gas card for the business; it's significant that your business as of now has a current credit report and scores built up. Most of all, enormous oil and gas organizations, for example, Shell, Chevron, and ExxonMobil require 3-4 exchange references on their business credit applications and will check your organization's business acknowledge report as a component of their credit basic leadership process. This additionally remains constant for suppliers that have practical experience in Þeet cards also, for example, Fleetcor, Fuelman, and others. Well, there you have it. Five different ways to construct your business acknowledge as quickly as would be prudent. Keep in mind, developing your business credit report isn't about what number of records you have announced.

Different factors, for example, installment action, installment history, size of credit limits, sorts of credit, what's more, length of record of loan repayment, all play a factor.

1. Register your business substance.
2. Get a business recognizable proof number (EIN)
3. Open a business banking account.
4. Set up a work locale and telephone number.
5. Apply for a business DUNS number.
6. Open exchange lines with your providers.
7. Get a business Visa or business credit extension.
8. Get from banks who report to business credit agencies.
9. Keep business data current with the authorities.
10. Pay the entirety of your business' bills and credits back on schedule.

If you've at any point been available for a buyer credit, for example, a home advance, you presumably have an idea about your funds. You know where your own FICO rating stands month-to-month, and how close to home credit impacts your capacity to meet all requirements for budgetary items. Be that as it may, as an entrepreneur, you probably won't know anything about your organization's business FICO score—why this is significant, what your rating is, or how to set up and construct business credit.

If you ever require credit for your business later on—with a private company advance or business charge card, for instance—at that point, your business can't only get by with a solid individual FICO rating. Your credit will help, yet you'll likewise need to assemble a positive business record of loan repayment. This being stated, in any case, before you can begin building business credit, it's imperative to comprehend the responses to the accompanying inquiries:

- What is business credit?
- For what reason is business credit significant?
- What are the advantages of business credit?

What Is Business Credit?

Before we jump into how to assemble business acknowledgment, we start with the fundamentals: What is business credit? Similarly that you assemble individual credit dependent on your monetary history, you set up business credit dependent on your business' money related history—which means how you handle any credit that has been stretched out to your business, including charge cards, advances, credit extensions, exchange lines from providers, and that's only the tip of the iceberg. Though close to home credit is attached to your standardized savings number, in any case, business credit is attached to your manager ID number or EIN.

At last, however, similarly, as your acknowledgment outlines your unwavering quality as a borrower, your business credit passes on whether your business is a reliable borrower.

How Does Business Credit Work?

Given this basic definition, we should clarify business credit in more detail and answer the inquiry, how does business credit work? As we referenced, one of the center's contrasts between business credit and individual credit is that business credit is attached to your EIN. In this manner, as you experience different monetary exercises through your business—opening a financial balance, getting a Mastercard, paying providers—this data turns out to be a piece of your loan repayment record and is accounted for by credit authorities that manage organizations.

The three principal business credit revealing offices are Dun and Bradstreet (D&B), Experian, and Equifax. Each organization gathers data from the merchants and lenders you work with, just as from legitimate filings also, open records. At that point, utilizing a credit revealing calculation, they set up your business credit as a numerical worth: your business FICO assessment. Dissimilar to an individual FICO rating, be that as it may, which is resolved based on a standard assessment strategy, your business financial assessment will differ dependent on the acknowledged agency as each office has its technique for figuring your score.

This being stated, be that as it may, your business financial assessment will generally extend from 1 to 100 with a higher score demonstrating that your business is trustworthy, which means you're probably going to cover a tab or credit back on schedule. Furthermore, albeit each credit authority has its assessment procedure, by and large, your business financial assessment will be impacted by components, for example,

Credit: Length of record as a consumer, credit use, credit blend, installment history, equalizations, and patterns

Segment subtleties: Business size, years in business, and industry chance

Open records: Amounts and recurrence related to liquidations, decisions, and liens

As you're attempting to fabricate business credit—particularly when you've quite recently begun your organization and are trying to assemble new credit—activities like paying on schedule, blending the sorts of credit you use, and not augmenting your credit limit will all profit your business financial record and in this manner, business FICO rating. Then again, activities, for example, missed installments, balances exceptional, and current decisions, would all be able to bring down your FICO assessment.

Now, you ought to have a away from how business credit functions. From the get-go in the life of your organization, you'll need to concentrate your time and consideration on building business credit. Although it requires some investment to get business credit, by assuming responsibility for your business' financial record, you'll begin to comprehend it more and perceive how, after some time, various activities influence your FICO score. Along these lines, in case you're thinking about how to construct business credit—and quick—there are some time tested techniques you can utilize. The entirety of the accompanying ten stages can affect your business financial record, and ideally, improve things.

1. Register Your Business Entity

As we've clarified, your business record is isolated from your financial record. Along these lines, the first venture to begin building business credit is to keep your business and individual funds and isolated. In request to isolate these accounts, at that point, you'll have to set up an enlisted business element Unincorporated business substances—a general organization or sole ownership—are the least demanding to work with in terms of firing up and overseeing administrative work. In any case, with these structures, there's no legitimate or money related detachment between the proprietor and the business. For this situation, when you decide to work with a merchant or apply for credit, you'll need to give your government disability number. Subsequently, your movement on your business records will be pondered in your credit report.

On the off chance that you need to set up business credit, at that point, you'll need to pick one of the accompanying structures:

C-partnership – A C-organization gives you and your business legitimate and money related detachment. Enterprises are viewed as independent legitimate urban communities. A C-organization is perfect for a business that is intending to issue stock or open up to the world later on. S-organization – S-corps go through elements in which business' benefits are just saddled at the personal level. S-corps are likewise viewed as independent legitimate elements. Constrained risk organization (LLC) – A LLC is another kind of joined business substance with obligation assurance and money related detachment among you and your business. An LLC is more uncomplicated to oversee than a partnership and offers more duty adaptability. Restricted risk organization (LLP) – A LLP is an enlisted business substance that is well known among proficient businesses, for example, legal advisors and specialists.

Even though it's critical to remember your capacity to assemble business credit while settling on your choice on how to structure your business, it's not by any means, the only factor you ought to consider. In case you're uncertain precisely how to pick the correct element type for your business, you can counsel a business lawyer or bookkeeper for help.

2. Get an Employer Identification Number (EIN)

The following stage to set up and construct business credit is to get an EIN. The IRS utilizes a business distinguishing proof number (EIN) to follow organizations for charge purposes. Much the same as your government managed savings number fills in as your distinguishing proof number for seperate charges, your EIN fills a similar need for your business.

For the most part, sole ownership organizations and single proprietor LLCs can utilize the proprietor's government disability. For the most part, sole ownerships, associations, and single-proprietor LLCs can use the proprietor s government managed savings number for charge purposes (as long as they don't have any workers). Most different sorts of organizations, however, need an EIN.

This being stated, regardless of whether you're not required to, it's a smart thought to get an EIN at any rate. Perhaps the most significant advantage of an EIN is that it can help you set up business credit. Also, an EIN is free and straightfoward to apply for on the IRS's site. At the point when you, in the long run, apply for an advance or a charge card for your business, you'll, for the most part, be asked to either give your Social Security number or EIN on the application. If you have your standardized savings number to offer, at that point, you can depend exclusively on your credit to assist you with qualifying and get a decent rate.

As we referenced before, on the off chance that you have an EIN, at that point, your business credit will be attached to this number, and you can utilize this history to meet all requirements for credit items and business financing.

3. Open a Business Bank Account

As we expressed over, it's fundamental to construct business credit, and all in all, to isolate your business and individual accounts. Notwithstanding picking your business substance, starting a business financial balance is an urgent advance to drawing a line between business and individual costs. By opening this record, business credit agencies will effectively have the option to perceive what cash you're removing from and placing into your business. They will report data on your business credit report.

Hence, when you have an EIN, you'll need to investigate your choices and open the best business financial records for your organization. After you open your record, it's imperative to utilize it. You should use this ledger to pay for operational expenses—

everything from utilities and lease to your business wireless. These buys, as long as you cover them and on schedule, without fail, can likewise add to building business credit.

All things considered, starting a business financial balance won't just give a bank reference to the three credit revealing organizations. However, it will likewise open entryways for better credit accounts later on—the best independent company loan specialists search for borrowers with business financial balances that have been built up for in any event two or three years.

4. Set up a Dedicated Business Address and Phone Number

Even though this next tip may appear to be a direct advance, getting a devoted workplace and telephone number will harden your business' various presence. This is a small, yet significant advance towards building business credit since it will permit you to enroll with professional references. To clarify, registries like the Better Business Bureau and Angie's List (https://www.angieslist.com/) expect organizations to have an address and telephone number to join. Business credit detailing offices gather data from these catalogs, so it's imperative to have the right and reliable contact data recorded on the entirety of the well-known catalogs.

Furthermore, when you set up a committed telephone line for your business, you're building up your first, straightforward exchange acknowledge relationship for the telephone organization. This history gets answered to credit offices and will help you build up business credit.

5. Apply for a Business DUNS Number

Of the three business credit authorities we referenced above, Dun and Bradstreet are presumably the most notable. Their Paydex score (https://www.fundera.com/blog/paydex-score) is the business financial assessment generally utilized by providers and banks. In this manner, on the off chance that you need to construct business credit, it's smart to open an acknowledge document for this organization.

To do that, you'll have to enlist for a DUNS—a Data Universal Number System. The DUNS framework is a numerical recognizable proof procedure for business substances. At the point when you apply for one, you'll get a remarkable nine-digit code. The procedure is free and can be finished on the Dun and Bradstreet site, yet it takes up to 30 days to get your DUNS number. Having a DUNS isn't a necessity for organizations, except if you're applying for a central government contract, award, or SBA advance, and it is anything but a framework that is overseen by the legislature. In any case, everybody from national to universal providers and banks utilizes D&B business FICO ratings, so if you're attempting to manufacture new business credit for your startup, applying for a DUNS is a smart thought.

6. Build up Trade Lines With Your Suppliers

If you've finished stages one five, at that point, you have just established a robust framework whereupon to build up business credit. To continue building business credit, at that point, there are some additional accepted procedures you can follow. One best practice is to keep up and set up great associations with merchants and providers. Similarly, likewise, with your credit, you'll assemble business credit as you expedite a wide range of providers, merchants, and moneylenders — given that you keep up a decent association with them. As you purchase more supplies, stock, or different materials from outsider merchants, those buys can turn into connections—and will, thusly, assist you with building business credit. As we referenced above, it will be especially helpful if your providers and sellers broaden exchange credit, which, to emphasize, implies they permit you to pay a few days or weeks after you get the things you requested.

Although this credit isn't originating from a customary bank, it is like an advance. Paying your merchant or provider on schedule and in full (perhaps even early), at that point, will assist you with getting great business credit—only like paying buyer Mastercards on time encourages you to manufacture your credit. For instance, Lucas Horton, a gemologist and proprietor of Valeria Fine Jewelry, said exchange lines helped his business credit: "I opened four reminder accounts with precious stone venders who answered to business credit agencies. Agreeing to Experian, my business presently has a B-rating (up from a D) because of the need for data. I am not huge enough to participate in things that would fabricate my credit [even further], like applying for a line of credit, so that is most likely as high as I will ever get. In any case, for my needs, it is sufficiently high to get me the credit I require.

A notice account is a point at which they send you precious stones, and you have a specific measure of time to pay for it instead of paying for it forthrightly. The majority of the more sizeable organizations I have accounts with at any rate report to Dun and Bradstreet or Experian."

This being stated, the key is to pick providers, as Horton did, who will report your installments to business credit authorities. Not all merchants do this, and on the off chance that your provider doesn't answer to the business credit organizations, at that point, your on-schedule (or early) installments won't assist you with building business credit. Along these lines, it's significant that the mainstream providers Uline, Quill, and Grainger all report to business credit departments. For whatever length of time that you cover on schedule and with these providers, you'll have the option to support your business FICO rating.

7. Get a Business Credit Card or Line of Credit

Numerous new businesses and independent ventures use advances and credit lines to fund the activity and development of their business. Not exclusively is this kind of credit critical for keeping a business running smoothly, yet utilizing it will likewise help with setting up and assembling business credit.

For instance, Nate Masterson, CEO of excellence organization Maple Holistics, said he depended on business Mastercards to improve his organization's business credit standing: "We chose to utilize business Mastercards in light of the fact that... they assume a fundamental job in building your organization credit profile. This is especially helpful for private ventures who depend on credits and awards. Moreover, in light of the fact that there are a few significant card backers which report your business action to your individual credit report, this can be an extraordinary method to help your own credit, in the event that you are dependable. Take care of your tabs early, or at any rate on schedule. This is the main, most significant guideline that will get your business an ideal FICO assessment with business credit department. We tried to just utilize our business card on buys we were sure we could cover off before every month's over."

Moreover, a business credit extension works similarly to a Mastercard, short the physical card. Instead, the assets live in your business bank record, and you can pull back cash-dependent upon the situation. You, at that point, take care of what you get to reset your balance. At last, the demonstration of obtaining and reimbursing assets on a business Mastercard or credit extension will help fabricate business credit—given that you're paying on schedule (or early, if conceivable) and in full. In case you're only beginning or have poor individual credit and are making some hard memories fitting the bill for ordinary business.

Visas, you can attempt to apply for and use verified business charge cards. A verified business credit card is "verified" by a finances store that you make against your card. In addition, on the off chance that you require gear, however, don't approach the important money or fit the bill for an advance, you may think about the advantages of renting. In addition to the fact that this allows you to get the hardware, you have to become your business. However, it likewise assists with setting up business credit.

8. Acquire From Lenders That Report to the Business Credit Bureaus

In case you're reimbursing your Mastercards and credits on schedule and in full, you can be glad for your outstanding installment history. Notwithstanding, you'll need to be sure that you're getting perceived for this great conduct and building business credit from your prosperity. In this manner, you'll need to ensure that you attempt to work with loan specialists who report to the credit authorities. In a perfect world, loan specialists should answer at least one of the three significant business credit agencies—D&B, Experian, or Equifax. Fortunately, this is, to a lesser, extent a worry with other monetary substances as most banks and customary financing foundations will routinely report borrowers' reimbursement narratives to business credit detailing agencies. Some online moneylenders, in any case, don't record reports to business credit authorities departments. To guarantee that you assemble business credit from an advance, at that point, you'll need to look into a loan specialist's approach before you apply.

9. Keep Business Information Current With the Bureaus

Every business credit department gathers distinctive data and has diverse scoring models. Over this, various providers and various loan specialists report multiple types of information. This being stated, because a loan specialist or provider could pull your business credit report from any or the entirety of the three principal agencies, it's significant that you watch out for every one of your reports—keeping up each of the three.

These departments permit you to refresh fundamental data about your systematic (the number of representatives or a long time in business) and transfer budgetary archives. The more complete your profile is at every one of the business credit detailing agencies, the better.

Also, and as we referenced over, it's critical to audit your credit reports from each of the extraordinary agencies, not exclusively to see your present status, yet in addition to guaranteeing that there aren't any mistakes influencing your business financial assessment. Indeed, even the littlest blunder can affect your business credit in an enormous manner.

In case you're not utilizing a constant credit announcing administration or observing instrument, a great general guideline is to check your business credit report at regular intervals. In doing such, on the off chance that you discover a mistake, you'll need to check that the data is genuinely off base, contact the suitable bureau(s) to clarify what is off ground, and solicitation that the vital change is made.

10. Acquire Responsibly

When you're pondering how to construct business credit, your mantra should be equivalent to building individual credit: get dependably. With consistent, mindful getting propensities—drawing from a blend of business credit accounts and covering those records on schedule and—you'll see your business FICO rating improve. Also, another factor you'll need to remember as surprisingly is your credit use proportion. Your credit use proportion is resolved on how much credit you have contrasted with the amount you're utilizing. For instance, you may have a $10,000 balance on $20,000 accessible credit—for this situation, and your credit use proportion is 50 percent.

Your credit use proportion is regularly a significant supporter of your business financial assessment. If you have a high credit use proportion, you are viewed as a more serious hazard. Consquently, you should endeavor to keep your credit usage proportion as low as conceivable to successfully fabricate your credit. For the most part, you should focus on 30% or underneath. In this way, in our model over, the half-credit use proportion is not exactly perfect. Similarly, another strategy you can use inside your obtaining to improve your credit usage proportion, what's more, in this way assemble credit is to expand your credit limit and not utilize it for the situation of a Visa or line of what's more, in this way construct credit, is to develop your credit limit and not use it. On account of a Mastercard or line of credit, when you've demonstrated to the loan specialist that you're financially sound (as a rule-following six to a year), you can demand a point of confinement increment, which will diminish your credit usage proportion. For instance, on the off chance that you had a parity of $10,000, however, your accessible credit had expanded from $20,000 to $30,000, your credit use proportion would decline from half to 30%, bringing you inside the perfect proportion and improving your business financial assessment.

Then again, albeit these tips will assist you with building business credit when things are working out in the right way, you likewise don't have any desire to overextend what you're able to do. Similarly, as with an individual FICO score, your business FICO score will languish if you apply over too many credit accounts over a brief timeframe. You'll need to make a point to scatter your business charge card or business credit applications. Furthermore, your business credit can likewise endure on the off chance that you have an excess of obligation, so you would prefer not to take on additional than you can deal with. You never need to make a late instalment, which is an immense factor in ascertaining your business financial assessment. Consequently, in case you're battling with income or experiencing difficulty taking care of your tabs as a consequence of an excessive amount of obligation, you'll need to consider alternatives like renegotiating or obligation solidification to make installments more sensible.

Why Building Business Credit Is Important

In this way, since we've clarified somewhat increasingly about how to manufacture business credit and how it functions, we should talk about why business credit is so significant. On the off chance that you maintain an independent venture, you may be thinking about whether it's worth putting resources into business credit by any means—wouldn't you be able to get by dependent on your credit?

Even though you actually could get by with merely your credit, it's geniunely not the best practice for little entrepreneurs. As we'll talk about beneath, there are certrain advantages of business credit, particularly excellent business credit. How about we separate the principle reasons why building business credit is significant:

1. Getting Small Business Financing

One of the fundamental reasons why it's so critical to manufacturing business credit is because your business FICO rating is a crucial factor in a bank's choice to work with you. Banks are probably going to expand an advance or credit extension to your organization just if they see that your business has a decent reputation of covering your records on schedule and. Moreover, on the off chance that you need to work with the best money lenders, it's considerably progressively huge to have set up great credit.

Also, when you apply for financing, not exclusively will a moneylender utilize your business record of loan repayment to decide regardless of whether to work with you; however, they'll additionally use it to determine how a lot of cash you fit the bill for—in truth, as indicated by the SBA, "organizations have 10 to multiple times more prominent credit limit contrasted with individual credit." Your business FICO rating will likewise factor into what sort of loan fees you get on your financing. For instance, in case you're applying to the SBA's 7(a) credit program offer the wellbeing rates available), the SBA will take a gander at one of your business financial assessments— your FICO SBSS— to prequalify you for the credit. On the off chance that your score is 140 or underneath, you won't pass their prescreen procedure.

Consequently, building business credit is significant for you to have the option to get business financing—and the ideal financing. Regardless of whether you're not searching for the funding in the prompt future, it's by and by essential to set up business credit. If you disregard your credit, a low score can constrain your loaning choices if you ever need subsidizing.

2. Supporting Relationships With Suppliers and Vendors

Almost certainly, you'll have to work with different providers and merchants to maintain your business. By and large, providers will offer exchange credit, the capacity to purchase now and pay later, to organizations when they're buying stock, material, hardware, and so on. Nonetheless, similarly, banks like to work with organizations with excellent credit. Providers are bound to offer you exchange credit if you have a reputation for taking care of tabs on time.

One of the advantages of business credit, in this manner, is the capacity to get exchange credit and get acceptable reimbursement terms. This being stated, not exclusively can exchange acknowledge help your business for income. However, it can assist you with building and keep up business credit too. If the organizations you work with report exchange data to the significant credit authorities, usually paying them on-schedule or early will help improve your score.

3. Ensuring Your Personal Credit

Finally, realizing how to assemble business credit and find a way to do it is significant since it will help you secure your credit. On the off chance that you have insufficient business credit, you'll likely need to utilize your credit to verify financing. Although that this may be a vital unfortunate chore during your business's early phases, it's never the perfect methodology.

One of the primary things any entrepreneur ought to do is independent of their business and individual funds, and along these lines, credit. Maximizing your Visas to finance your business can hopelessly harm your FICO ratings—which means if your business falls flat, you're left with poor individual credit, making recuperation troublesome. At last, building business credit—and when you're only beginning your business, constructing new credit—is fundamental for your organization's movement, development, and steadiness. Also, even though the idea of selling your organization might be the uttermost thing from your psyche, your record as a consumer will impact this procedure as well. The credit score of your business is entirely transferable, and subsequently, on the off chance that you sell the organization, the new owner(s) will profit from the work you put in.

What's in Your Business Credit File?

Numerous entrepreneurs are astounded to realize that they may as of now have a business credit report in their organization's name. Some credit departments, including Experian and Equifax, pull open record data, for example, assortment information and court records, to make your document and produce your score.

To see your business credit record, accordingly, you can apply online to get a report from any of the three significant announcing authorities. This being stated, be that as it may, every one of these organizations will charge you an expense to get to your report. Fortunately, there are a few spots online that you can use to check your business' record as a consumer for nothing. At Fundera, we offer credit checking, which incorporates a free synopsis of your business and individual financial assessments and will alarm you to changes in your credit reports. Furthermore, there are different administrations, such as Nav or CreditSignal, which will give you alternatives to see your credit record for nothing. Eventually, it's critical to perceive what your business credit resembles before taking any activity with the goal that you know where you stand and what the best subsequent stages will be to assemble or improve your credit rating. In a similar vein, by checking your credit document, you can check whether there are any slip-ups in your current credit history. Much the same as blunders on an individual credit report botches in a credit report can cut down your score.

In this manner, if you discover any blunders, you'll need to follow the procedure for every individual agency to debate the blunder and guarantee an amendment is made — the business credit report model.

Top Tips to Remember

If you've followed the ten stages we talked about already, you've figured out how to construct business credit—and ideally, have prevailed in really doing as such. Now, you're in the perfect spot to deal with your accounts, develop your business, and watch for your credit en route. In light of this, here are a couple of tips to recollect as to building credit as you proceed in the lifecycle of your organization:

Try not to depend on your credit. Utilizing your credit for your business longer than completely fundamental can harm your own FICO assessment and make it progressively hard for you to meet all requirements for any financing later on. Continuously take care of your tabs on schedule. Any late installment, even by one day, can harm your credit. Set up a framework to guarantee that you take care of your tabs on schedule. On the off chance that conceivable, pay them early. Check your score routinely. You'll need to know where your credit stands, and checking your score normally can assist you with perceiving how certain activities influence your record as a consumer.

Audit your credit reports for blunders, both enlightening and money-related. A Wall Street Journal study demonstrated that 25% of entrepreneurs who looked discovered credit-harming blunders on their reports. Make a point to check your reports for blunders and experience the procedure with the particular credit department to address them.

As an individual buyer, your credit becomes an integral factor now and again. For instance, your credit is a central point while applying for a vehicle advance, home loan, or Mastercard. A proper financial assessment will work in support of you, expanding your opportunity for prompt endorsement. On the other hand, a low score could keep you away from being affirmed. You ought to consider your business credit to be just as significant. Even though building business credit may not affect your own life, it can unquestionably represent the moment of truth in your organization.

This being stated, by exploring our ten credit-building techniques, just as learning the nuts and bolts of what business credit is, how it works, and why it's significant, you'll see it simpler to settle on educated and certain choices. In spite of the fact that it requires some investment to set up and assemble credit, it merits the exertion. At the point when you have a solid record as a consumer, it will work in support of you over and over.

The Most Effective Method To Repair Your Credit

Purchasing a house is the single greatest buy most purchasers will ever make—and most by far, individuals purchase that house using a credit card. Yet, home purchasing isn't the main time your credit is significant. Your credit is a factor when you need to lease a loft, purchase a vehicle, get props for your youngsters, or on the other hand to exploit a "no enthusiasm for a half year" offer on a widescreen television. Once in a while, your credit history will become an integral factor when applying for protection or occupation. Record of loan repayment assumes an imperative job in your everyday life, making costs like a home loan more— or then again less—costly for you. What's more, it isn't easy to lease a vehicle without a charge card.

It Is A Credit Economy

A developing number of individuals buy items and benefits using a loan—either with Visas or by taking out different customer credits. Americans obtain to purchase vehicles and trucks and put less cash down when they buy homes, as home costs rise in numerous pieces of the nation. In any case, Mastercards are the quickest developing type of shopper acquiring in the created world. What's more, they have the greatest effect on most shoppers' budgetary status. Mastercards are utilized by additional than 73 percent of American families, up from 16 percent during the 1970s. Most Americans have at least one broadly useful Mastercard nowadays, and all the more regularly, they have a few. By universally useful, we mean a Visa not given by a particular store or retail chain; these cards incorporate Visa, MasterCard, Discover, or American Express cards that can be utilized anyplace.

In particular, American Express observed a 13 percent expansion in cardholder spending from 2003 to 2002. Furthermore, that business was progressively productive. As per the organization, American Express Bank (AEB) revealed a net gain for 2003 of $102 million, up 27 percent from $80 million the year earlier. Visa, the biggest player in the broadly useful credit card showcase, created around $3 trillion in card deal volume worldwide every year in the early 2000s. Indeed, even Diners Club, a generally little player in the market, piled on net deals volume of $31 billion out of 2001. And afterward, there are supposed "hostage cards"— credit cards gave by retail establishments, corner stores, and claim to fame retailers. They represent something like half again the sum charged to the broadly useful cousins.

In principle, Mastercards permit you to make the most of your buys for up to a month before you need to pay a dime—and it's everything sans interest. Or if nothing else, it would be sans intrigue if individuals took care of their Mastercard balances in full every month. Most don't. As indicated by Fair, Isaac, and Co., which tracks customers' records of loan repayment, around 10 percent of Americans have charge card adjusts that surpass $10,000. Then again, about portion of the populace is significantly more moderate, conveying a parity of less than $1,000. (You'll peruse a ton about Fair, Isaac, and Co.— called by the abbreviation "FICO" by individuals in the credit and banking businesses—through the course of this book.). Mastercards aren't the main sort of credit customers use. As indicated by FICO, the typical purchaser today has 11 credit "commitments." Of those, seven are probably going to be charge cards; the other four are liable to be portion credits—including auto, home, and understudy credits.

On the off chance that you put it all together, you locate that 30 percent of Americans convey more than $10,000 of non-contract related shopper obligation. What's more, charge cards are the most signficant cut of that obligation pie.

Credit Gets Easier

Shopper credit is a kind of unavoidable outcome. As more purchasers use it, more dealers need to acknowledge it. Also, as more vendors acknowledge it, more shoppers use it. That is the reason it appears as though everyone needs to offer you credit nowadays. If you shop at an office store and pay with money or with a money order, numerous representatives have been prepared to request that you open up one of the store's charge accounts.

Creeping Effect

Credit has a relentless, total impact in transit individuals purchase things. The vehicle business is a genuine case of this crawling impact. Through the 1960s, most Americans paid money for their vehicles. On the off chance that an individual acquired to purchase a vehicle, the individual in question would, as a rule, make a vast downpayment (frequently a large portion of the price tag) and take a couple of years verified credit through a neighborhood bank.

During the 1970s, car producers chose to fund the acquisition of their items in a systematic manner. They promoted two-and three-year credits, which required littler upfront installments. During the 1980s, vehicle organizations began renting autos—which disposed of the upfront instalment; furthermore, the entire thought of a vehicle was something that somebody would purchase and keep for a long time. It likewise made extravagance vehicles increasingly reasonable to most buyers. To start with, leases had a multi-year term. Conventional advances stretched their standard terms to four or five years to contend.

By the mid-2000s, most Americans financed most of their new vehicle buys. Gone were the times of two-year automobile advances; five-year advances or rents had become standard—, and six-year advances were progressively normal. Supposed "extravagance" vehicles—which incorporated a few trucks—had become from under 10 percent of the vehicle market to more than 30 percent.

What Do You Owe?

Among the most upsetting measurements of late years have been how much charge card obligation Americans owe. As of March 2012: The absolute rotating obligation was $803.6 billion. The standard obliged family unit owed $14,517 in Visa obligation in excess of 46 percent of all family units conveyed some Visa obligation. These are huge numbers, and they might mirror your circumstances. Notwithstanding the Mastercard obligation, there are numerous different sorts of responsibilities. Among the most well-known:

- Home loan
- Vehicle advance
- Home value advance
- Understudy advance

Before we go any further, you have to know the aggregate sum of obligation you're as of now conveying. In Worksheet 5-1, show the aggregate sum you owe on Visas and store charge cards. Try not to compose just the least installments. Here's the reason: Suppose you owe $5,000 to a credit card organization, yet rather than saying that you owe them $5,000 this month, your bill says that you need to make an installment of $65. That is your regularly scheduled installment, isn't that so? Wrong. Mastercard and store charge card organizations are in the matter of profiting, and one route is by having you pay a high pace of enthusiasm on your obligation for whatever length of time that conceivable. Did you realize that if you make just the base month to month installment, you may be paying on that $5,000 for ten or fifteen years?

Also, that is without charging even one all the more things to your record, on the whole, that time! Paying just the base is never going to assist you with getting your money related circumstance leveled out.

Dr. T. Anderson

Your Income Far Exceeds Your Debts

Accepting you were straightforward in your appraisal of your pay and commitments, you ought to experience no difficulty building up spending you can live with. On the off chance that you can't concoct enough cash to pay the charges every month or your Mastercard obligations are developing, look at Part 4 to discover apparatuses for following your every day, week by week, and month to month costs to understand where your cash is going.

Your Income Just Barely Exceeds Your Debts

This means, on a yearly premise, you scarcely get by. In the event that you experience difficulty covering your tabs every month, you may have one of two issues. Either your costs are higher than you might suspect, or you may have income issues (talked about in the accompanying segment). Negative One to Negative Ten: Your Debt Just Barely Exceeds Your Income Many individuals live only a little over their methods. To do this, they use Visas, store charge cards, home value advances, momentary advances, etc., to make a decent living. The issue is that in case you're short $300 every month and use charge cards to pay for staple goods or attire, toward the year's end, you'll be $3,600 paying off debtors. After ten years, even with a Mastercard that gives you an OK loan fee, you'll be over $83,000 owing debtors!

Your Debt Far Exceeds Your Income

This circumstance regularly happens in the middle of times throughout everyday life. For model, when you're in school or have quite recently graduated yet can't discover a work, you're in the middle of living off your folks and working all day to pay your costs; however, you may even now have a similar spending designs that you had when your folks were paying every one of your expenses. You may likewise have a great deal of obligation because of a cutback or medicinal leave, or at the point when you have one gigantic obligation hanging over your head, for example, a school advance or surprising doctor's visit expense. See Chapter 10 for tips on managing squashing commitment.

6
HOUSE PURCHASING

You enter the commercial land center the minute that you purchase your first home. To buy that house, you have to have set your accounts up to have the option to pay your current bills just as any bills that are acquired in the new area. When you possess the property, regardless of whether you are getting it to flip or to live in, you are answerable for the utilities that are not charges identified with that house. Ensure you check out the market before purchasing. You need to correlate with making an offer. That implies that you can weigh up one speculation against another. A few people with less cash to contribute may decide to select a house that necessities fix over a longer timeframe. The way that the house is in an awful condition of fix will imply that the cost available will have been moderately lower; however, the stunt is working out what the home would be worth once these fixes are finished what's more, what the expense of those fixes is prone to come to.

Value is the measure of cash that property gives you, like the potential for another advance on a property. If your property was purchased for $100,000 and is as of now worth $150,000, at that point, you have a value of $50,000, or you may find that your loan specialist would be glad to progress that sum, contingent on how persuaded the loan specialist is that the estimation of the property would become to ought to you default on your installments. There are various scales that you need to recollect too. The market esteem may contrast from a valuation of the home for bank purposes since every one of the banks need to know on the off chance that they will get their cash back. The market esteem, be that as it may, might be adaptable contingent on changes in the market. For instance, if there are relatively few houses available to be purchased, at that point, the house is more important because it's an irregularity and something that individuals will be looking for. On the off chance that there is a lodging surplus and there is an excessive number of decisions, at that point, it's likely a fast-moving business sector, and you may get less for your home. The other valuation you have to remember is the valuation for protection objects is entirely unexpected from the past sorts of valuation. This ought to be founded on what it would cost you to supplant the house if it was devastated. An insurance agency will have the option to give you a valuation to know what protection is probably going to cost you.

On land, you have various kinds of deals. Short deals are when you can purchase a property at not exactly the sum that the dealer owes to the bank. For a situation like this, the bank may have abandoned ever getting back the sum owed and may concur that the dealer can offer to pay off as much as the house will probably figure it out. The issue with short deal costs is that they don't generally end up being as brilliant of a house as the buyers figure it will be. There might be fixes required that are unreasonable; however, buyers hop in indiscriminately because they sense that they are getting an incredible deal. A home examination costs cash, yet it doesn't cost as much as the potential misfortune that you can make on the off chance that you purchase a short-deal property that necessities more consideration than its value.

Sale properties – These are, for the most part, properties that have been dispossessed on. The current proprietor can't stand to pay the home loan, and the bank needs back the cash that is owed. We will go into this afterward, yet essentially these are houses the bank is set up to sell for the sum owed on a particular date. The favorable position of these businesses is that you can get deals. The inconvenience is that you need to have examined the property in a short space of time and ought to have the financing set up before you offer. The botch that individuals make with this sort of procurement is that they provide over their financial limit and leave less cash for fixes.

Deals through realtors – These are houses that have been put on the showcase for an assortment of reasons. Perhaps the proprietors are moving to another town. Maybe they are just moving to a bigger home. On account of seniors, these seniors might be moving into helped living and needn't bother with a considerable home anymore. There can be a wide range of reasons a house goes onto the market. The bit of leeway of this sort of offer is that you can typically discover the foundation of the house and have additional time wherein to explore and settle on the worth of the home. You also have more bartering power because the land operator will contact you, what's more, the dealer.

For rental speculation, the inconvenience is that it ties up your underlying cash and except if you have more cash for your next speculation, this may not be a decent move. In any case, if you have overabundance money to contribute, you may find that you will be ready to recover any home loan installments from inhabitants, which implies that the venture pays for itself over some time.

Budgetary Decision

When you enter the land advertisement, you have to realize the amount you can stand to spend. This ought to incorporate the cost of the home just as the legitimate charges, specialist's expenses, adequate cash to revamp the house varying and put it back onto the market. When you possess the house, it will pick up no pay and be a risk. Subsequently, your financial limit must incorporate a fixed timeframe where you will be expected to pay the home loan while any work required is being finished. Individuals frequently disregard this part of the cost, yet consistently that you possess the house will cost you cash and ought to be checked.

When you are settling on your financial limit, remember what the bank is arranged to offer you and what this will cost you during the time you possess the property. You also need to guarantee that you can manage the cost of mortgage holders' protection for the period that you possess the property and realize what duties apply to your proprietorship. You should have a distinct top on what you can stand to spend because this permits you just to extend and a little higher, remembering that there is continuous space for exchange. It serves to have the option to get a temporary worker to give you introductory statements on the expense to do any fixes on the property. Renovating can be costly yet essential to raise the estimation of the home or to fix things in the home that should be in acceptable working request. Contingent upon the work that requirements to be done, you may need to counsel with handymen, circuit testers, or merely broad temporary workers to get the best statements and thoughts for redesigns.

I would state to any individual who needs to get into this business that you should be genuinely mindful of normal fixes cost. For instance, I have a rundown of current costs that I allude to when looking at new properties:

- The expense of reworking an essential three bedroomed house
- The expense of overhauling a two bedroomed loft
- The expense of introducing a kitchen into X measure of square feet
- The expense of supplanting guttering
- The expense of supplanting slipped shingle or tile
- The expense of introducing a subfloor over X measure of square feet
- The expense of evacuating asbestos

- The expense of disposing of form over a set measure of square feet

Before you even consider venturing foot into a house, have an organizer assembled with sensible costs that are speculative be that as it may, which give you a thought of what you are taking a gander at. The sorts of employments that you will have the option to utilize incompetent work for are the underlying tearing out of old things from the property and preparing it for contractual workers. You should know what day rate somebody charges on the grounds that frequently this sort of work is done on a day rate. Be that as it may, be cautious. Ensure that your concept of a day is equivalent to theirs.

Different costs that will come into the picture are things, for example, dumpsters. In the underlying phases of possession, these will spare you a great deal of time. You have to know about a neighborhood organization that can convey one on a quick turnaround and evacuates it when you need it and the expense for such work. Different ways that you can eliminate your spending limit is to set up accounts at your nearby stores with the goal that you are qualified for limits for provisions, blunder, installations, what's more, other redesign needs. This will help you to set aside cash. Developer's stores that sell dry dividers and the entirety of the things required for the renovation ought to be ready to offer you a credit account. This permits you to spend plan for the costs instead of having sticker stun at the expense of provisions per trip.

Be educated

You may locate that a few enhancements to houses will be qualified for awards, and you should know about this since working inside the rules given can spare you a ton of cash. See whether this just applies to your main habitation or, on the other hand, whether awards are accessible for houses that you plan to sell. You, too, need to know from a bookkeeper or somebody who can let you know what capital additions charge applies to houses. These standards will assist you with working out what your spending plan is and what you are liable to make from a house. When you examine houses, know that in the zone where houses are found, there might be a lot of houses available to be purchased. On the off chance that this is the situation, take a gander at the challenge. See what homes are selling and for what cost. Getting agreeable with a land specialist will help you suppose that you will give them your business, they will be glad to furnish you with data.

There are a few things that you have to consider when you assess a home. These are as per the following:

- How the house contrasts and others available in a similar zone
- How the value contrasts and different houses
- What the home offers
- What inconveniences there are

Release me into this in more detail since right now, you may not be acclimated to the lodging market. On the off chance that this is your first venture, you have to get it right. The first of the criteria is truly evident because investigating different homes inside the zone will give you a thought of what the market resembles. On the off chance that you are taking a gander at a family home, is the zone in which the house is found appropriate for family life? You have to comprehend what's accessible and what costs what's more, regardless of whether the home can fill some hole in the market.

Family homes need:

- Access to great schools
- Safe avenues for children to play
- Good vehicle joins
- Good shopping offices

The official settlement would require different things:

- Up to date and present-day convenience
- Nearness to ship joins
- Parking
- Availability of night diversion in the zone

Various types of individuals need unique things. Knowing the market that you're going into is significant. On the off chance that your showcase is immersed with family homes, the official lone ranger cushion may not be the best choice, and you may wind up losing cash on the exchange.

What weaknesses are there?

The minute you enter a home, you ought to be searching for issues. Are the floors strong, or are there regions that squeak? Are there fixes that were never wrapped up? What is the stylistic theme? Do the kitchen and restroom need supplanting? Are the floors in the property in excellent condition? In what state is the woodwork ready? Is there a twofold coating, what's more, if so, to what standard? Is there an off-road stop? How much work will be done before the house can be put onto the market, and what will the fixes cost you?

You are in an ideal situation, going into a home with your eyes open to the entirety of the detail. If you notice old electrical attachments hanging off the divider, odds are you may need to rework the house. If the tile is broken, why? If this is on an upstairs floor, you may need to supplant the tile, yet the subfloor it is sitting on is likely the purpose behind the breaks. You should be an investigator to a certain degree.

Take a scratch pad or clipboard and note everything that you see. Take a camera, focuses, and shoots pictures of anything you are in question about with the goal that you can examine this with temporary workers varying, at the point when you have assessed, if you are genuine about making a buy, never part with your cash before you have evaluated things accurately and do get a property evaluation that features any of the things that you may have missed. These are finished by experts who recognize what to search for.

Making an offer

There are a few things that will tell you that somebody is so edgy to sell a home. Signs that there is space for exchange in the value are the following:

- The house has been available for quite a while
- The house is estimated too exceptionally contrasted and different houses in the region.
- There are fixes to be done that will be expensive.
- The proprietors have just moved out so are frantic to break joins with their previous existence.
- The home has been disregarded.

These are primarily incidental things, yet they provide you some insight about the property; what's more, they also reveal to you whether the home is probably going to sell at its current cost. The realtor will have the option to let you know if the price has been dropped as of late. They will likewise have the option to converse with you about the conditions of the merchant. Be benevolent. Learn as much as you can since the entirety of this data can help you to get a deal.

At the point when you have your property report, you will have the option to make a progressive point by point appraisal of what it will cost to do any remodels that might be required, even though that may not prevent you from making an offer. Suppose there is a great deal of enthusiasm for the home. In that case, you might have the option to make a speculative offer, remembering the fixes you have just noted with an arrangement that the request depends upon an acceptable property report. That covers you in the event that there is something extreme that you didn't get on when you were checking out the house.

If you are managing to purchase the house through a realtor, you ought to never make the offer directly with the dealer. Talk things through sensibly with the realtor. For instance: "Considering the measure of fixes expected to get the house up to date, I might want to propose an idea of $ X sum subject to a good property report." The realtor will have been working with the vendor and ought to have a smart thought of whether your offer comes anyplace close to the sum that the merchant needs. You get more data from realtors since selling the house is their fundamental need.

In any case, don't be talked into something that your sense lets you know is a higher cost than you are set up to pay since you will remain to lose more. The typical technique is for the realtor to contact the merchant and return to you either with a counteroffer, which you can leave from, or subtleties of what the merchant is prone to acknowledge. When you are making offers on houses, you may find that you are left with this feeling of expectation. Try not to phone once more. It shows the realtor that you are excessively sharp, and that is not a decent thing. On the off chance that you show the entirety of your cards, you leave yourself powerless, and it's not justified, despite all the trouble. There will consistently be another house and another probability. Try not to be convinced to pay more for the home than you feel it is worth, remembering the checks you have done against other houses and the measure of fixes you would need to do to get the house up to a similar condition are selling for more cash. The more you part with at this stage, the less possibility you have of turning a benefit. At the point when you are searching for a house to live in as opposed to flip, you should, in any case, look from a business perspective. This is presumably the most extraordinary speculation you will make in your life. At a later stage in life, you might need to sell it on. If it takes you an outright fortune to get it into shape, you may not recover your cash on it, and it's not worth getting yourself into that circumstance in any case. If you have questions about the expenses and are being pushed to make a higher offer, leave. Make sure of what you are getting into, and try not to sign anything until you have all of the realities and are content with them.

Restoration

When you realize that you are going to purchase a property to flip, you also need to know the timescale for the work that requirements to be finished. On the off chance that you are new to the procedure regarding the property, you have to land the entirety of your position offers from circuit repairmen, handymen, drywall specialists, and whoever else will be doing to work to get the house into the ideal condition. There is a set-request to work, and if this isn't regarded, you will discover it costs you more to complete things.

Beginning arrangement – If you have plans about what you will do to the house, you will know whether interior dividers need wrecking or on the off chance that you need a kitchen tore out or a washroom tore out. The underlying readiness stages are done by somebody who is a worker, and these individuals, for the most part, charge you a daily rate. It is my experience that you have to be as active as conceivable to spare you cash. Keep in mind, in the event that you leave somebody who is on a day rate to their gadgets, they may extend the activity basically to procure more. If you are there during this time, you can ensure that this doesn't occur.

This underlying arrangement needs doing before you have qualified contractual workers into the property since it's essentially getting all the terrible stuff out. You might be ready to set aside cash in certain zones. For model, the kitchen units might be acceptable quality and have a great deal of life left in them, be that as it may, you might need to supplant the entryways of the units. At this underlying stage, you need to have continuous notes with the goal that you can request the entirety of the things that you need so that they are there when your certified laborers need them. It costs you cash to have temporary workers hanging tight for building materials to be conveyed.

First fix – This is the phase that occurs before dry divider is finished. This incorporates things like fixing subfloor issues, evaluating the harm you may have found while tearing things out, and so forth. You may have discovered spoil, and maybe there is asbestos that should be expelled from the property. You can't do this work. You should ensure that a qualified individual comes in and does it. Pipework and wiring that goes behind dividers are done at this stage. You will need to plan handymen, circuit testers what's more, different temporary workers to come in stages so they won't be competing for the equivalent spaces simultaneously. This time will likewise incorporate monitoring what lighting should be introduced to bring the house up to current models as all the wires should be laid prepared for this.

Second fix – This incorporates the entirety of the things, for example, dry divider increases, tiling, what's more, the things that you will consider such to be kitchen worktops, fitting kitchen units, ensuring that every one of the attachments is placed in place. Ensure that you know when tilers will do their work because this should be done related to the kitchen or washroom fitting and are significant. Additionally, you would prefer not to do floors when you know there is still untidy work to be done except if you are ready to secure them completely. To keep this composed, ensure that you use a spreadsheet. Regardless of whether you don't realize how to utilize an expert one from your PC, in any event, make a posting that shows the entirety of the dates what not of the occasions that you need laborers to be at the house with the goal that you can plan everything, and it runs efficiently.

A potential misstep you can make here is having temporary workers on location before they are required. This costs you extra cash in light of the fact that regardless of whether they are sitting around sitting idle, you are getting charged for them being there. You may consider this to be outlandish. Notwithstanding, if you booked them in to begin a vocation and they are there, however, the structure materials are not, you are as yet liable for their time.

Requesting a considerable number of materials that you require for the house must be done in advance. Attempt to work with off the rack things as much as you can because anything that is made to gauge will cost you extra and may set aside more effort to be conveyed, and this can cost you extra cash.

Ensure that your temporary worker's statements are comprehensive and that they are separated so you can drop things off the rundown if essential to keep your financial limit in trim. Try not to alter your perspective and having additional things. It is much better to make an exhaustive arrangement for your renovation instead of include things at a phase that will cost you extra cash. Ensure likewise that your contractual workers are accessible on the dates that you need them to be and that they have been secured to a completing date since this gives them the impetus to take care of business furthermore, leaves you comprehending what arrange the remodel will be at, consistently during the remodel of the house.

DO IT YOURSELF

There might be approaches to set aside cash during the remodel of a house. If you are attempting to stick inside a financial limit, it's a smart thought to try the accompanying ideas to assist with setting aside your cash. On the off chance that you have abilities that you can utilize, you can spare a fortune. Here is a portion of the ways that you can attempt to set aside cash.

Working – During the underlying tearing out of the old apparatuses and fittings, it doesn't take a great deal of aptitude, yet it takes numerous hands! On the off chance that you are there and ready to oversee, you can likewise help with a few of the employments, for example, tearing out old kitchen and restroom fittings. Working isn't that difficult. It's only an instance of getting associated with the everyday procedures that are going on at the house. This encourages you to minimize your expenses. For instance, tearing out an old tiling or taking out an old washroom is not unreasonably hard. However, they need doing. On the off chance that you can free yourself up to help with this, you will be setting aside cash. Help with contractual workers – When you approach contractual workers for their statements, do enquire as to whether there is whatever you can do to help out and to make the costs a little less. There may likewise be work that they are glad for you to contribute to, which can set aside cash. On the off chance that you feel that you are ready, you can presumably do this similarly just as he can; what's more, set aside your cash. Be straightforward and forthright about your spending limit and attempt to prevail upon the support of your temporary workers. Regions that you can help with might be all the enrichment that requirements are doing toward the finish of the activity. If you feel that you are capable, at that point, it will be advantageous to do it. Assuming this is not something you are acceptable at, at that point, make sure that you can help by making the clearing up and arrangement to set aside cash. Don't hinder the temporary workers; however, show that you are happy to get your hands grimy if it encourages you to keep your work inside the spending that you have set.

When you begin to get out of your first house, you will find that there are continuous things that you can do to spare cash. You can be nearby while the work is being performed and will be ready to ensure that you are getting things done accurately and in a convenient way. When every one of the contractual workers has completed their work, the real arrangement and completing contacts make that house sell. Individuals need to see nonpartisan insides don't as well, make the house excessively beautiful. They need to be ready to envision their lives inside that home. If that implies that you can utilize any of the current fittings inside a house, it's less expensive for you to enlist a sanding machine than to supplant flooring. It's less costly to take off organizer entryways and supplant them yourself than to introduce another kitchen.

The contractual workers you indeed can't hold back are circuit repairmen, handymen, woodworkers, and roofers. In any case, having a top-notch craftsman accessible, you might have the option to compromise utilizing their ability. They may likewise be willing to work with you and welcome your connection with them during the work. Toward the day's end, it's your venture. You are the customer, yet you ought to never get so nonchalant about the work that you think yourself above doing any of the physical work yourself. On the off chance that you get into this state, and I have known individuals who have, you will spend more on your work than had you moved up your sleeves and taken every necessary step yourself. Time costs cash. For the individuals who are happy to contribute to the work, there are numerous ways that you can spare. You can likewise make yourself accessible to assist when you see that temporary workers need you; however, make sure to ask ahead of time. A few temporary workers work quicker when they are left to it, so finding a workable pace character of your temporary workers is basic. Be inviting, furnish them with something to drink as they work, and attempt to make a relationship that functions admirably for both you and them.

7

REAL ESTATE WHOLESALING

This picture discloses to you a great deal about what we're going to talk about in this first section. "Wholesale" brings to mind the conventional significance of the term, for example, retail activities (like Costco or Sam's Club). The distributor who carries items to the market needs to purchase their stock at a massive rebate from advertising worth and sell the stock at a markdown, so the end purchaser feels they got a decent arrangement. The "spread" between the two costs is the place the distributor makes its benefit. In any case, with retail wholesaling, there is a very expand set of overhead structures and expenses.

Wholesaling land is the point at which a land distributer puts an upset home under agreement with the expectation to allocate that agreement to another purchaser. The distributor doesn't anticipate ~xing up or selling the property. Instead, they showcase the home to potential purchasers at a more significant expense than they have the property under agreement. In case you're looking for a home value credit extension, you can contact each loan specialist, in turn, trusting you find a decent bargain. You can then visit an online commercial center, like LendingTree, and audit offers from numerous loan specialists on the double. Spare time, shop keen and find a HELOC that fits.

What Is Real Estate Wholesaling?

Land wholesaling is the procedure through which an individual, the 'distributer,' obtains an agreement from the property vendor and doles out that equivalent agreement to an end purchaser. Wholesaling is viewed as extraordinary compared to other momentary venture procedures. What's more, it is an extraordinary path for people to break into the land contributing industry. This is because wholesaling doesn't require massive funding to begin.

A distributer can make a benefit by recognizing properties being sold for under market esteem, settling on concurrence with the merchant of the property, and relegating the buy agreement to another purchaser. They procure income through a wholesaling expense connected to the exchange — regularly a level of the general property cost. End purchasers are ordinarily land rehabbers or different sorts of financial specialists who favor not to invest energy recognizing limited properties or haggling with merchants. By going about as the go-between, wholesalers create salary by helping land financial specialists find and close potential arrangements. Be that as it may, there are a few things to remember to make wholesaling function admirably, examined straightaway.

So How Does Real Estate Wholesaling Work?

Real estate wholesaling works for individuals who are happy to place in a lot of sweat value. While it is moderately hazard-free, wholesaling requires a lot of due perseverance and exertion to see a solid return. Maintaining a wholesaling business can be testing since you should have the option to distinguish properties being sold for well under market esteem, arrange manages dealers, and target money purchasers who are happy to buy those properties. To be effective in wholesaling, you should be set up to put a great deal of exertion in building solid lead records, just as systems administration and curating your discount purchasers list after some time. The individuals who are eager to ace the procedure in such manners make certain to encounter the advantages of wholesaling land.

Similarly, as with retail wholesaling, when you discount land, you're the centerpiece between a spurred merchant and a money purchaser, making your benefit from purchasing low also, selling somewhat higher. The significant contrast is that you're not shipping or store stock or ever spend cash to try and secure your stock! The way to wholesaling land is "control." At the point when you place a property "under agreement" for procurement, although you haven't finished the exchange yet, during the end time frame, you basically "control" the land as per the "terms" of the understanding you made with the motivated vendor. Also, since you "control" the property, you may now lawfully showcase it to discover a money purchaser ready to pay more than the value you consented to pay to the inspired vendor. The spread between the two costs is your benefit as the distributor. You will get paid the distinction when the end money purchaser, in reality, closes on the exchange. We will get into detail later about structure your rundown of money purchasers who will buy your accessible discount properties. These are typically either fix and flip financial specialists (likewise called rehabbers) or long haul rental financial specialists (likewise called landowners), who will be glad to purchase from you. This permits you to procure a decent benefit as long as you can convey properties beneath showcase esteem.

In another part, we'll discuss how you find troubled properties, roused vendors, and homes accessible at profound limits to current worth. When you have a money purchase and a limited property, and if the numbers work to benefit the center, you're prepared to do a discount bargain. Why would that be a spot for you in the center? By what means can there be a benefit accessible when the vendors could interface straightforwardly with the purchasers? This is continuously done.

The fundamental reasons are because most money purchasers are lethargic and either doesn't have any desire to set aside the effort to discover a dealer willing to sell at a large enough discount...or they do not have the comprehension (instruction) to have the option to find and haggle excellent arrangements. As the land advertise changes (moves from a purchaser's market to a seasonally tight market or the other way around), discovering bargains on the MLS (Multiple Listing System) may turn out to be progressively troublesome. At the point when this occurs, money purchasers can't depend on land operators for discovering bargains. That is the point at which they go to wholesalers for crisp venture openings. Your most noteworthy esteem is in your capacity to find upset properties or troubled individuals and haggles to purchase at costs well beneath advertise esteem. You find properties your financial specialist clients aren't mindful of arranging a price to acquire/control the property; at that point, offer it to your speculator purchaser at a value that is beneficial for the both of you.

The most effective method to Wholesale Real Estate in 7 Steps Wholesaling land is an extremely momentary contributing methodology. A few people mistake it for fixing and flipping. However, there are fundamental differences. Wholesaling land is beneficial if you need to get into land yet don't have a ton of money, yet defeats can remember perplexity for its lawfulness and confusing agreements. Here are the seven stages of how to discount land:

1. Locate a Distressed Property to Wholesale

Troubled properties are commonly best for wholesaling because they can be acquired under market esteem. Upset properties are those in deterioration or those with proprietors who are roused to sell rapidly. Finding a troubled property will empower you to sell the property for more than what you put it under agreement for.

Since part of the intrigue of wholesaling land is the low capital necessities, those new to wholesaling land will commonly search for nothing or reasonable approaches to find upset properties. Prepared speculators will have other intends to find upset properties, which we examine underneath. Three of these hotspots for finding upset properties are land discount and land venture gatherings, online land destinations, and utilizing the administrations of a collaborator. Land Wholesale Groups and Real Estate Investment Groups Land discount and land venture bunches are composed of gatherings between nearby realtors and financial specialists. They're an incredible open door for new wholesalers to connect with realtors, title organizations, temporary workers, and appraisers. You may meet lead sources, accomplices, and even coaches. These clubs convey week after week messages with accessible properties available to be purchased. This data can enable you to comprehend what is being purchased and sold, the amount they're selling for, and what neighborhoods have stock. This knowledge will be significant later on when you apply it to your own wholesaling business. The properties in the email incidentally originate from realtors, yet most are properties that troubled merchants have gone over to wholesalers to sell rapidly.

You can find neighborhood land bunches by doing a snappy google search, joining a Meetup bunch in your city, or joining a Facebook or LinkedIn gathering. Contact your neighborhood Chamber of Commerce and inquire whether they have any up and coming land financial specialist gatherings. There are likewise online registries that rundown nearby land speculator bunches, which you can contact legitimately.

No Cash, Credit or mallets required

Numerous individuals need to get into land contributing because we've all been told it's probably an ideal approach to manufacture wealth. As it may, there is a typical misguided judgment you need the money and a great credit to bounce into the game. This is simply Not True! As you'll get the hang of wholesaling doesn't require cash or credit since you're not expressly going to purchase the property. Your job is indeed to be the center man in the exchange that brings the merchant and purchaser (financial specialist) together. The assets expected to purchase the property will originate from the purchaser you allocate the agreement to, so again, you'll never require money, credit, credit extension, or home loan endorsement to be a land distributer. Notwithstanding wipe out any hazard, all the land contracts you'll use in wholesaling contain "leave provisos" that permits you to escape the agreement should you have issues ¦nding a purchaser to allocate the agreement to.

Real Estate Sites for Wholesalers

Land destinations are an extraordinary spot to find troubled properties; however, you have to know which ones to take a gander at. You need to use locales where propelled vendors can post their properties. You can find these inspired merchants and their bothered properties by looking on craigslist, FSBO, and HomesByOwner.com. When utilizing these locales, type in the city or area you are searching for and think about using watchwords in your ventures, when accessible. Catchphrases will limit your inquiry, so you are finding the most spurred vendors, accordingly the best arrangements. Some well-known watchwords include:

- Motivated agent
- Distressed property
- Fixer-upper
- Sold as it stands
- Must sell
- Estate deal

Contract a Property Finder

Another famous and affordable approach to find bothered properties is by utilizing a collaborator to help you locate these properties. This property finder will find properties that you can conceivably discount. They will distinguish these arrangements by scouring neighborhoods, thumping on entryways, and cold pitching property holders. This right hand won't be an hourly representative and won't be paid forthright. Instead, they may be paid when you buy one of the properties they found, and it goes to settlement. The land business term for this sort of partner is a fledgling canine. The name is gotten from the canine that chases for flying creatures, similarly as the associate chases for property bargains.

A flying creature pooch can be found in understudies hoping to profit, and occupation load up promoting destinations. They assume a fundamental job in wholesaling because they will spare the distributer such a tremendous amount of time finding properties. This time spared can be placed into different business zones, for example, finding purchasers and interfacing with various financial specialists.

Different Methods of Identifying Distressed Properties

After you have finished a couple of land discount gives, it is ~ne to evaluate different techniques for distinguishing bothered properties. Three standard techniques incorporate setting up desperado signs, mailing, and working with a realtor with some expertise in speculation properties. These strategies require some investment and need forthright capital. You should designate a few thousand dollars to get scoundrel signs made and set up. These signs are intended to pull in home dealers who need to sell their home for whatever reason and select not to go the customary course of utilizing a realtor. Making and mailing out advertising flyers, letters, and postcards are another approach to urge bothered vendors to get in touch with you. With the goal for this to be an effective system, you have to realize who to send them to. You can purchase on the web mailing records or utilize direct mailing administrations, which take every necessary step for you.

Another frequently ignored approach to find upset properties is via looking at probate court records for late acquired properties. You can see separate from court records and open duty records to recognize past due mortgage holders. When you incorporate an ongoing show, you can send them flyers or letters, including your contact data, and notice that you purchase properties in any condition. It is additionally critical to refer to you to pay money.

The last asset for distinguishing bothered properties is the assistance of a realtor. A realtor can help you find a property; however, remember, most realtors are not happy with the discount procedure. It is best to utilize a realtor who is likewise a distributor or get a referral from another land distributer or other land speculation bunch individuals. The realtor commission should be figured into the price tag of the home as well. Realtors will avoid wholesalers since they want to utilize their own agreements, and land specialists feel increasingly good with the standard agreement they are as of now acquainted with. Realtors need to present a decent confidence store when making an offer on the house, and since wholesalers would prefer not to set up their ash, they frequently skirt this progression. Realtors don't feel great with doling out agreements because the property is being sold twice, and the property holder is uninformed of this. By and large, realtors feel like the wholesaling business is circumspect, and their notoriety will be spoiled on the off chance that they are related to it. Realtors are authorized and protected and need to maintain the code of morals they attempted.

Make an Offer and Convince the Owner to Sell

When you've recognized a property, that is a decent arrangement, and the time has come to persuade the landowner to offer the property to you and sign your agreement. This progression is significant in light of the fact that it will determine how you secure properties to discount and make a benefit.

Approach the Owner

When moving toward a property holder, it is essential to go about it sensitively. Since a distributor isn't a traditional realtor, they should pick up the property holder's trust before pushing ahead. This can be done by being proficient, considerate, and on-time when meeting the mortgage holder.

Make an Offer and Get a Low Price

When the mortgage holder has consented to meet with you, you'll need to examine the benefits of offering the home to you. Most wholesalers center around how offering to them will lighten whatever torment focuses are rousing the dealer in the first place. A model may be helping somebody abstain from defaulting on a home loan they can no longer afford. Wholesalers will likewise accentuate how they will deal with the agreement, a property examination, the evaluation, and the shutting process. This won't put any extra weight on the mortgage holder since these things are being dealt with. Numerous wholesalers will feature the way that the property holder won't have any forthright expenses. It is additionally essential to educate the mortgage holder regarding the property fixes that should be done to fix up and lease or exchange the house. This is significant because the cash spent on fixes will legitimize the offer you make to the property holder.

Marking

The property holder should sign your agreement. You can utilize the assistance of a nearby lawyer or realtor; however, most wholesalers compose their agreement, modify a conventional land buy agreement, or use a wholesaling understanding format. They do this to include their conditions and don't need to cling to the entirety of the statements in a standard Understanding of Sale. This will be examined all the more later in the article. Most wholesalers tell the landowner that the purchaser is, actually, their accomplice. They do this, so the proprietor doesn't have the foggiest idea that they're relegating the agreement and making a profit. Although this is legitimate, from what our lawful specialists have let us know, it's most certainly not suggested because it's tricky. They enlighten the vendor regarding an accomplice, who is the assignor. This individual is who they offer the arrangement to. That way, they can show the site to them and let them know not to talk business as indicated by Sherman Toppin, PA Attorney, what's more, Real Estate Broker.

3. Discover a Title Company, Contractor, and Appraiser

A land distributer needs a title organization, a temporary worker, and an appraiser in their group. These experts add a degree of polished skill to your group and help your whole discount exchange run all the more easily. Every expert will set aside you time and cash over the long haul. An appraiser that you work with can turn out without prior warning give you an examination for the property you mean to discount. This will guarantee you are following through on the correct cost for the property and have space in the cost to exchange the agreement and make a profit. An accomplished purchaser will likewise need to see an examination before buying the property.

A title organization guarantees the purchaser is purchasing a real bit of land. They run a title search on the property to check whether there are any liens on it. The title organization will be utilized at settlement, and they should be financial specialist benevolent. This implies they are open to managing allocated contracts, which we will get into in a later area. Try to ask them this forthright and speak the truth about your expectations with the property.

Finding a dependable, sensible temporary worker or proficient jack of all trades goes far around here. The temporary worker can accompany you to take a gander at the potential property and draw up a gauge of fixes. You may not figure these issues since you aren't repairing the property and are selling it in 'as is' condition, yet it is useful when you discover a purchaser. Each of these experts can be found through referrals, online inquiries, and proposals from a genuine home wholesaling gathering. Another land distributer will have the option to disclose to you who he suggests utilizing in your general vicinity.

4. Evaluate Property's Renovation Needs

By evaluating what remodels a property needs, you know the expenses and guarantee they fit your arrangement to profit off the bargain. A troubled property that requires remodel implies a higher edge for the financial specialist that you offer the property to. This higher edge will permit you to profit off the arrangement also.

You can give the gauge of fixes that your contractual worker drew up to the purchaser, so they realize what's in store. They won't have the option to make you too low an offer dependent on overrated fixes because you comprehend what fixes need to be completed and their cost. Having this gauge of fixes is a vital arranging device and will increment your general profit.

Recognizing what remodels the property needs and the amount they cost will likewise give you a thought of how many the ARV of the property will be. This is especially imperative to show financial specialists to see the worth and potential profit that your specific property will bring them.

5. Discover a Buyer

You found a property to discount, have the fundamental experts set up, and realize what fixes the property needs. It is currently time to find a purchaser. This won't be a first-time home purchaser or a family; yet rather, it will be a financial specialist or, on the other hand, a contractual worker who will purchase and fixing the property. Finding a purchaser is significant and should be done rapidly since there will be a settlement date on the agreement, which should be clung to. When you are first beginning wholesaling, you might not have a rundown of purchasers; however, you can find them in an assortment of ways. The absolute most cost-effective spots to find purchasers include:

- Publicizing the property on free sites, for example, Craigslist and Zillow.
- Circulate flyers with the property data on it all through the area
- Email speculators that you have met at financial specialist meetup organizing occasions with the property data

When purchasers begin calling about the property, spare their name and contact information, regardless of whether they aren't keen on this property. You can make a snappy spreadsheet or utilize client relationship management(CRM) programming to spare all of this data, and this will be your purchaser's rundown. Each time you have another property at a discount, you can send it to your purchaser list. This will diminish your promoting costs, thus expanding your potential profit.

6. Arrange a Deal with the Buyer

When you have discovered an intrigued purchaser, the time has come to arrange an arrangement with the purchaser. This arrangement is essential since it will decide how much cash you make o{ the arrangement. Your profit will be the difference between what you acquired the property for and what you're wholesaling the property for. While haggling with the purchaser, utilize the contractual worker's gauge furthering your potential benefit. Tell the purchaser that you have different purchasers intrigued, and on the off chance that they need to get this incredible property, time is of the quintessence. The purchaser should leave a great confidence store, which can be made out to the distributor or the title organization and held bonded until the property goes to settlement. At the point when you are haggling with the purchaser, ensure the entirety of your expenses are secured.

Appraiser charges Contractual worker stroll through expense Title charges, on the off chance that you paid them, to get a head start on the title search Any showcasing charges including what you will owe your birddog guarantee that after your expenses are secured, you will make enough profit to make the procedure worth your time, effort and gas cash. Most wholesalers expect to make at any rate $2000 profit of each discount bargain by and large. If you aren't making that sum, the arrangement does not merit doing. Most wholesalers figure a flat expense, yet ARV is as yet significant for the financial specialist, as is examined in the Numbers area later in the article.

7. Shutting on the Wholesale Property

The end, or settlement as it is additionally known, will occur at the title organization's o|ce and will last around an hour and a half. All gatherings will meet up, and the deed will be moved to the new proprietor. When this is done, it will be the consummation of a discount bargain. The end date will be referenced in the agreement you marked with the landowner and the deal you kept with the new purchaser. The purchaser will pay every end cost and the merchant except if it concurred and the new purchaser will get keys to the property. You picked a speculator cordial title organization that will lead the end to keep all gatherings satisfied. Since there were task conditions in the two agreements, the distributor will, by and large, not move the property into his name. This individual, generally a financial specialist, will place the property in his name, or almost certain his organization's name. This is an approach to stay away from paying exchange imposes on two separate exchanges.

The Philadelphia Department of Revenue and most Pennsylvania regions have been alarmed by twofold exchanges.

They think about every exchange, even a task, a property move that should be burdened. The City of Philadelphia has been getting serious about wholesalers, as Sherman Toppin, PA Attorney and Real Estate Dealer, indicated.

Is real estate wholesaling right for you?

Wholesaling is directly for individuals who need to get into the land; however, they don't have the financial intends to do so. It is too useful for individuals with an eye for bothered properties and solid arrangement abilities. Wholesaling will take a great deal of time in any case; it can receive significant benefits whenever done accurately. To begin in the land wholesaling business, you have to play out some examination. You should find land speculator bunches where you can pick up guidance. You will likewise need to put the time into finding troubled properties and propelled vendors. Ultimately, you should get acquainted with the wholesaling contracts. If you like to meet new individuals, have the land energy, and have solid relational abilities, you may consider getting into land wholesaling. For a great many people, it is their first invasion into the land. This is the situation since it doesn't require a land permit or any instructive prerequisites. Contrasted with other land fields, it moreover requires less of an underlying financial venture.

As you figure out how to discount land, you will start to acknowledge whether you're equipped to deal with it or not. There is plenty of hazy areas; what's more, it requires a vast time responsibility to find the properties and find purchasers to buy them. When you do not many gives, you will be increasingly acquainted with the agreements, the showcasing procedure, and finding bothered properties.

Having this information will give you the confidence you have to prevail in serious business.

Is Wholesaling Real Estate Legal?

Wholesaling land, when all is said in done, is legitimate. Wholesaling real estate includes finding a troubled property and afterward making an offer on it. The request will be dependent upon you, offering it to another financial specialist. When the financial specialist buys the property, a discount arrangement will be finished.

There are numerous segments to know about. Rules and guidelines fluctuate by state, so it is useful to go to a neighborhood genuine home venture bunch for counsel. Likewise, it is fitting to put in two or three hundred dollars and counsel with a genuine bequest lawyer in your general vicinity since there are such a significant number of hazy areas. Contention encompasses the task of some portion of wholesaling. This is when a distributor gets a property under agreement and offers it to another financial specialist for a task expense. Numerous individuals believe it's unlawful because it's handling land without a permit. Be that as it may, it's legitimate in MD and DC, as indicated by Brian Pendergraft, a lawyer at The Pendergraft Firm. What is lawful for wholesalers to do in one purview may differ, starting with one then onto the next.

Wholesalers frequently target individuals in abandonment with post office based mail. The Maryland Protection for Homeowners in Foreclosure Act (PHIFA) keeps individuals from speaking to that they're "helping the mortgage holder in forestalling a dispossession if the aftereffect of the exchange is that the mortgage holder will never again possess the property."

The 'stop abandonment' post-office-based mail pieces that wholesalers convey in DC and Maryland may be modified to be consistent with Maryland law as indicated by Brian Pendergraft a lawyer at The Pendergraft Firm.

What You Need to Know About Wholesaling Real Estate

You have to know however much as could reasonably be expected about wholesaling land. You should know where to find purchasers and instructions to compute the numbers, so you profit. You will likewise need to understand how the allotting procedure functions and what to remember for an agreement.

Where to Find Buyers

Knowing where to find purchasers is significant because they are the individuals who will buy the property and profiting. These purchasers will be seen from land destinations, showcasing flyers, and signs and from land speculator gatherings. Most wholesalers begin with the free destinations, for example, Zillow and Craigslist. The next movement is going to speculator gatherings and workshops to get direction on where to search for purchasers and likewise check whether any of these speculators are keen on acquiring your property.

At that point, you will utilize advertising materials that rundown these properties available to be purchased. They can be posted in broad daylights that see a parcel of track and sent to neighborhoods you are focusing on. These materials will tell the perusers what a decent bargain your property is and that you have numerous others in different regions available to be purchased.

Inevitably, you will have finished a couple of discount land extends and will have many purchasers that you reliably work with. You will find a good pace and their inclinations. You can search for properties that they need to purchase, dependent on what they enlighten you concerning their local inclinations, style of home, and contributing methodology. This is likewise an incredible method to get familiar with the business by working with prepared financial specialists. It is less dangerous than seeking a purchaser to show up as well.

Step by step instructions to Calculate Wholesale Profit

Ascertaining the numbers on a discount land bargain is significant because it will decide how much profit you will make. The profit is the general purpose of the discount business. To find a good pace, you will likewise need to know some other significant numbers, including ARV and remodel costs. The arrangement needs to bode well for the land distributor and still leave space for the financial specialist, otherwise called the purchaser, to profit. Here's a basic condition to utilize, so you make in any event $2000 as a discount expense off of each bargain. The Contract + Estimated Rehab Costs + $2k Wholesale Fee ought to be < ARV. The purchaser needs to have space to make in any event 15% of the arrangement. Deciding how you will earn cash is the premise of your wholesaling business. You will make cash by buying upset properties at underneath showcase esteems. You will, at that point, offer them to financial specialists for more than you paid. The financial specialist will purchase from you since they, despite everything, have space to profit on the property on the off chance that they decide to fix and flip the home.

Doling out a Real Estate Wholesale Contract

Doling out a land discount contract is the way toward obtaining property from a mortgage holder and allotting it to a financial specialist before you purchase the property. This is done to diminish the forthright costs that wholesalers need to put out to buy a property. Wholesalers will utilize their agreement to incorporate specific language and provisos, which are to their benefit.

The ~rst proviso will give the distributer an out on the off chance that they can't sell the property. It says that if you haven't found a purchaser or an 'accomplice' as the agreement words it, you are not committed to buying the property. This dispenses with the danger of coming up with the cash for the property on the off chance that you can't find a financial specialist.

The second proviso that wholesalers incorporate is tied in with appointing the property. They include a provision that expresses that they can discount the property to anybody or any business and that the merchant doesn't need to know about this. This permits the distributor to sell the agreement and not need to put out the cash to first buy the house. When relegating an agreement, it is prescribed to be as transparent as would be prudent. If you aren't an authorized lawyer, don't offer the vendor or the legitimate purchaser guidance about the agreement. Additionally, avoid speaking to yourself as a business on the off chance that you are not authorized as one. This implies you don't talk to the other side more than the other. Remain impartial, and counsel a lawyer if any inquiries emerge. Rocket Lawyer is legitimately made straightforward. They give contracts, affordable access to lawyers, and fast online procedures for enlisting your business.

How Do You Know The Right Price To Buy?

To comprehend what you can pay, first, you have to realize what your money purchasers will pay. You work in reverse from the value you can sell through your expenses and wanted benefit, and afterward, you comprehend what you can pay. Your purchasers are ordinarily astute genuine domain financial specialists who know their business sectors and understand what wanted returns they are searching for. They realize what a decent arrangement resembles and make a fast purchasing choice once they locate a proper arrangement. Regardless of whether they're fixed and flip or long haul rental financial specialists, you can be sure that they have a decent handle on their expenses and the benefit they need from their ventures. One more thing you can wager on is that they won't have any desire to pay full an incentive for a property. Effective financial specialists need to purchase beneath showcase worth and lock in some benefit from the principal day of proprietorship.

When, Where, and Who Can Wholesale Real Estate?

Before we get into the "how" of land wholesaling, we should move beyond the uncertainty and dread that numerous individuals have when they're beginning another business. Land contributing can appear to be confused with money related boundaries to section. Different feelings of dread have to do with whether you can be fruitful in wholesaling on the off chance that you make some full memories work, are in school, or no doubt about it "numbers" type. Shouldn't something be said about where you live; will it work there? Considerably more terrifying to some is thinking about whether you're entering the business in an inappropriate blemish ket, timing is wrong. This section is about the when, where, and who of genuine domain wholesaling.

When Does It Work?

We've all experienced the land and home loan emergency that started in late 2006 and the prior decade when it appeared as though you could make cash purchasing a home with your eyes shut. Utilizing the period from 2000 through 2013, we can see each period of a land cycle.

Dr. T. Anderson

Upswing

During these 13 years, we saw a massive upswing, with costs rising at a quick clasp going into 2005 and 2006. Land flipping was amazingly famous because it was geniunely gainful. Financial specialists were getting one month and selling at a benefit the next. It was a fantastic time for land speculation. All in all, shouldn't something be said about wholesaling during that period? Consider it also; you'll comprehend why it was a brilliant time, no doubt domain wholesalers. There were boundless benefit openings, and rehabbers were energetic money purchasers of just about anything you brought to them. The distributor needed to find pretty much any property they could get "under agreement," regardless of whether it was at only a minor rebate to current market esteem. It didn't appear to make a difference if the rebate was little because the quick value thankfulness at the time implied that the money purchasers were anticipating a pleasant benefit, regardless of whether they proved unable to procure their flips a profound rebate. The speed at which a rehabber could turn home at a decent benefit implied that they were continually watchful for more arrangements. They utilized themselves to purchase, revamp, and flip whatever the number of properties could reasonably be expected.

Downtrend

At that point in late 2006, the market changed direction quickly. Plunging qualities and costs left many property holders owing more on their home loans than their homes were worth, and abandonments spun out of control. This opened up a HUGE chance for speculators. During the downtrend, there was a whirlwind of purchasing going on. Over 30% of every home buy being made with money financial specialists were from 2008 through 2012. In 2013 that number hopped up to 43% as per RealtyTrac.com. Wholesalers had a significant influence in settling the market and satisfying interest for limited properties by thinking of innovative techniques to discount short deals, bank possessed properties, abandonments, and government possessed houses (HUD houses). Likewise, during this time, major institutional speculators hopped into the fight, with flexible investments like Blackstone Group purchasing a considerable number of homes as investment property interests in significant urban areas. And keeping in mind that they obtained a large portion of their stock from dispossession barters, they likewise acquired numerous houses straightforwardly from land wholesalers! Indeed, even as of 2015, wholesalers are the go-to source numerous rehabbers, landowners, and even speculative stock investments go to when looking for their next speculation opportunity.

Sideways Market

This kind of market is spoken to by, for the most part, stale home value development; however, there can be moderate value appreciation. It's a more incredible amount of an all-encompassing arrangement of good and bad times with no broadened development in either heading. Numerous states in the mid-west and littler urban areas around the nation that didn't experience the significant slope or decay of house estimations during the blast/bust encountered a sideways market and still do to this day.

The fascinating thing about sideways markets is that there is still interest in venture properties and numerous roused vendors hoping to sell fast for money. There are multiple reasons why somebody would need to sell quickly for cash in a sideways market. Employment misfortune, demise in the family, movement, ailments, lawful issues, confronting abandonment, tired of being a landowner, cutting back/upsizing, the house needs an excessive number of fixes, separate, and some other explanation under the sun that could cause a money related hardship.

In conclusion, sideways markets are to a limited extent because of low interest and fewer purchasers. When that is the situation, on the off chance that they're not purchasing, they should lease. More leaseholders mean higher rents, and higher rents pull in more money investment property financial specialists. More financial specialists mean open doors for wholesalers.

Altering Strategies To The Market

The makret's pattern status is unimportant in case you're an instructed land distributor with significant business and promoting frameworks. Property types, value ranges, and neighborhoods of the properties sought after will change. Yet, there there will consistently be money financial specialists needing to place their cash into the land to purchase n-hold or fix-n-flip. The methodologies and procedures you utilize just should be acclimated to fit the present market cycle. You'll realize what you need to know in this book to do that. Wholesaling is considered by numerous individuals to be the most adaptable land venture specialty just because it works in each market, no matter what direction it's drifting.

Where Does It Work?

Presumably, probably the best motivation to discount land is the way that it works in numerous areas. Substantial urban areas and little towns. For whatever length of time that there are mortgage holders and houses...wholesaling land is conceivable. And keeping in mind that you may have heard the expression "area, area, area" as the brilliant standard for land financial specialists, there are many money overwhelming landowners and rehabbers that adoration owning or flipping houses in lower salary regions as much as they love doing it in the best neighborhoods.

Another magnificent motivation to discount is the way that it can be done both locally and remotely. To that point, simply comprehend that as long as you have remarkable frameworks set up for producing and changing over roused merchant and money purchaser leads, and an extraordinary group of neighborhood individuals set up to support you, you can discount genuine domain.

Who Can Be a Wholesaler?

What are the training necessities to be an effective distributor? Shouldn't something be said about monetary necessities? Would you be able to work full-time and still discount land? Shouldn't something be said about family duties and keeping up an ordinary way of life while you construct your business? These are generally substantial inquiries, yet you can't let any of them stop you or moderate you down.

Time, Family, and Lifestyle:

In case you're similar to the more signficiant part of us, the exercises of our bustling lives tend to occupy the time we have accessible. Families require some serious energy, our occupations) require significant investment, and what little we have left is ideally getting us a touch of unwinding or excursion time.

If you keep a log of your day by day exercises, you would effortlessly observe how much time you are spending and what assignments. At that point, you could begin to organize your time and spotlight on the ones that are generally critical to you. At the point when I did this, I found that I was burning through a vast amount of significant time concentrated on "non-cash making exercises," and even though I made some full memories work, there was still a lot of time every week to concentrate in on my passion for contributing. All in all, what amount of time will land wholesaling take? The answer is diverse for every individual, and it will differ depending on your present objectives and assets. A few people have full-time employment and work for their contributing organizations on evenings and ends of the week. This should effortlessly be possible for whatever length of time that you set up the privileged business and promoting frameworks to assist you with certain robotizing pieces of the business. For example, you can have your inbound calls replied to by a replying mail or go to a phone message. At that point, you could have a remote helper ($3.00 - $6.00 hr.) screen the calls and just put you in contact with really inspired vendors or money purchasers. There are even land contributing programming frameworks like the M5 Automated Marketing Machine that can auto-mystically create and catch up with your leads on autopilot. Once they arrive at a point where their low maintenance wholesaling pay is more than their all-day work salary, they stop and do wholesale full time. Others that don't have another activity invest as a lot of energy as vital to accomplish their monetary objectives snappier. Neither one of the ones is a set in stone decision; however, get this, your joy and accomplishment as a land distributer is going to be founded on three things:

1) **Finding enthusiastic help by whatever methods available.**

a) This implies you encircle yourself with similarly invested business people that offer a similar sort of monetary. What's more, way of life objectives as you do. Now and then, this can be testing, particularly if your loved ones "downpour" on your contributing procession. When I first began, my family disclosed to me each reason "why" I should keep my "genuine" work. It took them seeing me start to get fruitful before they began being strong. Fortunately, during that hard enthusiastic time, I had an astounding tutor to help manage and bolster me when I required it most.

2) **Take little strides towards BIG objectives. It's o.k. to think** beyond practical boundaries and set high money related objectives for yourself. Yet, you must concentrate on (and commend) all the "little successes" you will experience while working out your wholesaling business. Creating your first lead, breaking down your

first arrangement, setting your first arrangement to meet with a vender, strolling your first property, arranging and making your first offer, getting your first arrangement under the agreement, adding your first purchaser to your money purchasers list, wholesaling your first arrangement, and yes, cashing your first check. It's the little "wins" en route that add fuel to your contributing enthusiasm and help drive you towards your more significant objectives.

3) It's about the way of life you need.

a) There is no other activity that I have ever known about where you can make $10,000, $20,000, even $50,000, or on the other hand, more on a solitary exchange. Fabricate your wholesaling business around the way of life that you need for yourself. On the off chance that you are essentially attempting to acquire some additional cash to take care of off tabs or put something aside for retirement, at that point, you would set-up and work your wholesaling business uniquely in contrast to on the off chance that you depended on your wholesaling salary to endure. Spend some time thinking about "why" you need to discount land and assemble your business around what you truly need, both genuinely and truthfully.

Training Factors

A higher education won't exclude you from land wholesaling. O.K, that was a joke. Be that as it may, all joking aside, you needn't bother with higher education or even a land permit to discount land. Truth be told, probably the wealthiest and most effective wholesalers I realize scarcely graduated secondary school! Try not to misunderstand me; you require training, just not the conventional sort you might be utilized to.

Money related Requirements

With regards to private land contributing, you indeed just have two or three alternatives. You can discount, you can fix-flip, or you can purchase n-hold. While fixing and also flipping as owning rentals requires loads of money to finish the exchange, wholesaling expects next to zero cash since you are utilizing your back-end money purchasers' cash to finance the arrangement. Yet, that doesn't mean you needn't bother with any money to be a distributor. Having a business telephone, a PC with web access, and enough cash for your sincere stores will be required. What's more, for those of you that don't have the foggiest idea what a geniune store is, basically consider it a modest quantity of cash you give the merchant as a store to "hold" the property during the end time frame. In additional proficient terms, it's the "thought" a purchaser gives the dealer to affirm the agreement. I have utilized as meager as $10 as a sincere cash store and as much as $5,000...it's whatever you and the dealer consent to.

Looking at this logically, two or three hundred dollars for sincere cash can get you into an agreement. Utilizing free advertising strategies like "driving for dollars" can reveal a persuaded merchant. At that point, a free promotion on Craigslist could draw out a money purchaser searching for a decent arrangement. There's much more detail to come; comprehend that your prosperity isn't needy upon your bank balance!

Proceeding onward since you're persuaded: This part ought to have convinced you that there are no high jumps in your way to practical land wholesaling. A considerable number began with wholesaling to procure fast money at that point utilized a portion of the cash they made to put resources into rentals, what's more, fix-n-flips for more generous paydays and wealth building. Your money related objectives are inside your compass! Presently we should get into the "instructions to" of getting it going.

The Cash Buyers List

I referenced before that we're going to begin from the last part of the wholesaling process finding money purchasers. We will need to do this for two reasons. The first explanation is on the grounds that your money purchasers will help instruct you on what's happening in the market by mentioning to you what kind of legitimate ties they are searching for also, what neighborhood they need to buy bargains. The second explanation is because discovering money purchasers to add to your Celebrity purchasers list is an action that should begin today and never end. Every day you need to coordinate with potential purchasers. That way, when you do have accessible discount properties, you will know precisely which money purchasers to coordinate your properties to.

Finding Cash Buyers

Fortunately, there are financial specialists out there stacked with money and an incredible want to claim land. There are two significant classes for the financial specialists you'll be pursuing:

- • Fix and Flip: These financial specialists are in the matter of taking bothered, appalling, and additionally issue properties, remodeling and fixing them, at that point offering them to long haul financial specialists or retail purchasers. You'll be progressively forceful in finding bargains well underneath ARV (After Repair Value) since the fix-n-flip financial specialist will likewise need to make a benefit.
- • Long-Term Rental Investors: These speculators need to purchase a property underneath advertise an incentive in a useful territory for rentals and at a value that will permit them to acknowledge incredible positive income after some time. It might be more testing to find prepared to-lease properties than bothered ones; however, offering to this gathering is more straightforward and takes into account a pleasant net revenue. Presently how about we find a good pace viable manners to find, meet, and construct associations with these money speculators. Some are free, and others may cost a couple of bucks, yet until you have a decent purchaser show, you ought to convey the same number of these systems as could reasonably be expected!

Real Estate Investment Clubs

There are numerous reasons why you ought to think about joining a nearby land venture club. You'll gain so much from their library of materials and visitor speakers, just as from your individuals. Individuals incorporate realtors, different financial specialists, genuine domain lawyers, bookkeepers, contract representatives, fix contractual workers, fabricating and redesign temporary workers, title organization staff, home protection operators, and property the board experts. These individuals are essential contacts and conceivable future colleagues for your developing land speculation business. For this exchange, be that as it may, we're keen on meeting different financial specialists who could be possibilities for our purchaser list. There will be experienced speculators in these clubs who are there to search out arrangements and individuals who can bring them bargains, as it were you.

Be that as it may, there will likewise be amateur speculators who are there to learn, and they may have no considerations of wholesaling or fix and flip. They're individuals tired of 3% returns on bank accounts, what's more, declarations of the store. They've been presented to rental property contributing, and they need to find out additional. These amateur speculators offer an incredible chance to share information, present yourself as a distributor, and to clarify what you do and how you can assist them with achieving their objectives. It's a successful win if you can secure a productive property for an investment property financial specialist new to the business. By helping them arrive at their income objectives, you're assembling a relationship that can prompt different buys later on.

It is anything but difficult to locate the land venture clubs in your general vicinity. Go to Google and look for "YOUR CITY or STATE NAME, land speculation club." You will locate the most forward-thinking connections to your neighborhood venture clubs, so you would then be able to click in and investigate further.

Smart In-Person Networking Tips:

The following are a couple of face to face organizing tips I needed to share with you before proceeding onward to the following money purchaser system. At whatever point you are organizing face to face, you ought to consistently be arranged and never "take a blind leap of faith." Proceed to get some expert business cards made with your name, work title (proficient distributor), and PDA. At whatever point you go to any expert systems administration occasions, I recommend recording and remembering your "30 Second Business" before you go. This is your lift pitch of what your identity is and what you do. Keep it short, sweet, and to the point, and make sure to concentrate your pitch on how you "advantage" others. For example, you may state, "My name is Cody also, I spend significant time in helping land financial specialists simply like you reveal profoundly limited lucrative chances to either fix and flip or purchase and hold. I am an incredible advertiser so I continue running into off-advertise bargains that you can't discover anyplace else. I couldn't imagine anything better than to get familiar with what your identity is also, what you do so I can bring as a lot of significant worth as I can to our relationship. So...tell me about yourself how did you get into land contributing"?

The objective is to get the individuals you are organizing with to do most of the talking. Individuals love discussing themselves, and they will appreciate organizing with you in the event that you give them a stage to flaunt! As a last little tip, attempt your hardest to recollect people's' names. While this might be hard to do, I propose hefting around a little scratchpad or envelope and a pen at whatever point you go to a systems administration occasion. This way, when the discussion is finished, you can write down a snappy note about the individual, when you plan on following up with them, and how you trust you can profit them.

The genuine enchantment occurs after the systems administration occasion is finished. It happens when you ring the individual and approach them out for a mug of espresso or lunch and find a workable pace outside of the systems administration occasion. No one can tell where that relationship will lead. They may turn into an extraordinary money purchaser to add to your Celebrity money purchaser list, a private cash loan specialist ready to loan you money for your fix-n-flip arrangement, or a potential tired proprietor needing to sell an issue property.

Bandit Signs

You've seen these small, plastic side of the road signs at road crossing points, around parking garages, and different spots where property holders drive by all the time. They are there since they work. In this part, we're not discussing property holders, notwithstanding. That is in the following section. We're going to discuss how outlaw signs can draw in real money speculator purchasers. Rather than the signs saying something like "I purchase houses," or "Money for your home," switch up the message on your sign to discover purchasers. You need your criminal signs to look like they were made by a mortgage holder edgy to sell their home or some other dealer attempting to sell modestly. The thought is to draw in a money speculator purchaser who is spurred to purchase and close rapidly on a great arrangement. It's a decent wagered that an approach one of these signs in a certain neighbor-hood implies that the speculator was driving that zone searching for circumstances. Presently you know where they have an enthusiasm for purchasing, so all you need are a couple of more subtleties, and you can begin a relationship that could be entirely beneficial well into what's to come.

Recall that we're moving toward our wholesaling as though we're money poor, so we truly need a money purchaser before we find a property and lock it up for an arrangement. It's definitely not misdirecting to put out these signs, although that the financial specialist who calls may understand they weren't, no doubt. When you have them on the telephone, they ought to be eager to listen for a minute they need on the opportunity that you will convey it.

Grouped Ads

Similarly, as the desperado signs, you're not going to get the measure of results you need by running a promotion that says, "Money speculators needed." Instead...you need to pull in them with the correct lure.

Utilizing a portion of similar procedures and substance, you're running advertisements that present an extraordinary worth home available to be purchased at a markdown in a decent neighborhood. You can utilize a more signficant number of words than on a little criminal sign, and the promotion will, in any case, for the most part, be economical. You should run them reliably and in a similar area in the classifieds. Financial specialists will become accustomed to seeing them, and sooner or later, you may get that cash call. When you get the call, you do likewise, telling them it sold. However, you have others in the pipeline. Ask what they also need, where, and their value criteria so you can check your properties for a match.

The fundamental thought here is that you truly need to act once you get a lead this way. You don't need to perform medium-term; however, you should be back in contact soon with your progress and more inquiries if important. Hence, before you run these promotions or spot those signs, you ought to have started statistical surveying and have some forthcoming homes on your radar. You can quit fooling around once you have a purchaser in the wings. The screen capture from Craigslist demonstrates the immediate way to deal with discovering money purchasers, just as helping us to delineate the intensity of the online hunt. This was a straight inquiry in the classification "land needed" with the catchphrase "money." We're quickly observing promotions run with money land financial specialists forcefully looking for homes. Or on the other hand, this is likewise valid, perhaps wholesalers utilizing advertisements like these to find homes for a deal at a profound rebate to esteem. You won't know which until you contact the individual who set the promotion. On the off chance that it is a distributer, just a couple of moments of your time is squandered. On the off chance that it's a genuine purchaser, you have a chance. Running advertisements to sell a house at beneath evaluated esteem is another methodology, similarly to what we talked about for crook signs furthermore, arranged promotions. Craigslist is extraordinary in light of the fact that it's free, and you can be increasingly expressive without it costing you cash. This inquiry was in "land available to be purchased" with the catchphrases "underneath examination." We'll examine this again in the section on finding properties. For this section, we are also observing that we can advertise to sell a home at a genuine worth cost to check whether we can pull in financial specialists with money.

An accommodating element in online quests like these is the "autocomplete" work. At the point when you begin composing in a search query, the site will show you different inquiries with the word(s) you've composed in them. These are looking through others have utilized. Along these lines, beginning to type "must" will get you "must sell," and perhaps other recommended phrases. This can assist you with looking through you might not have considered previously, yet they're being utilized by purchasers and dealers. Craigslist is an incredible asset, as it's well known and free. The main drawback is there are con artists, so the approach was making contact with any individual who reacts to your advertisements with care.

Site or Blog

Having a site or blog includes validity to your land contributing business and enables you to produce online money purchaser leads. Quite a while back, I would utilize WordPress (a blogging stage) allowed to download; however, it took some specialized aptitudes to set-up. I became weary of all the muddled things I would need to do so as to have a high change over the lead creating site. Things, for example, purchasing area names, obtaining facilitating, contracting a visual fashioner and a web software engineer, composing duplicate (the words on the website page), and so forth. I chose to make my own lead assortment programming that completed two things incredibly well... make multi-page sites and single page crush pages with the snap of a catch, at that point, channel those leads into a promoting framework that emails, message, and direct-to-voicemail voice broadcasting. I considered it the M5 Automated Marketing Machine. It permits a non-well informed individual (like me) to in a flash have an excellent wholesaling website(s) (where I can show my accessible properties) that naturally manufactures my money purchaser list since the site is enhanced to rank high on web crawlers.

The illustrations are now accomplished for you. The duplicate is as of now achieved for you; the subsequent messages and messages are as of now done for you (the framework trickles out messages and messages to new leads auto-mysteriously assembling an association with the leads for you). I even composed a free digital book you can offer to tempt potential money purchasers to join your VIP purchasers list. Everything is accomplished for you, so you don't need to consider anything. Simply get the framework, and you will be ready for action within 24 hours. What's more, the coolest part is that any leads you to gather utilizing the M5, naturally, channel into an email advertiser, and a book message advertiser. It even channels into some cool innovation that permits you to send a voice message to anybody on your rundown that sidesteps their telephone ringing and gets saved legitimately into their voice message inbox! So at whatever point you get a discount property under agreement, you can just log into your M5 and impact out the property to all your money purchasers by means of email, content, as well as voice communication. The money purchasers take a gander at the arrangement and ring you to get it. It indeed can be that basic IF you have the correct innovation in your business!

Social Sites

Online networking can be a period squandering movement except if you get centered and send a particular methodology like producing money purchasers. The primary informal community that appears to work the best for discovering money purchasers is LinkedIn.com. LinkedIn.com is an expert interpersonal organization where you can, without much of a stretch, discover land contributing intrigue bunches just as different gatherings centered around a particular entrepreneur or calling. I propose joining bunches for "Specialists," "Bookkeepers," and "Dental specialists." These working experts typically gain extraordinary cash and may require an approach to contribute it! The way to progress on Linkedin is to take as much time as is needed and be locks in. Not at all, like systems administration face to face, web-based systems administration takes some time longer for individuals to feel good with you. Invest the energy essential to assemble compatibility with the individuals of your gatherings, and once you have done so, then beginning acquainting them with your wholesaling business.

Influence Your Power Team Members

Your speculator, well-disposed realtor, shutting specialist, property supervisor, and land lawyer presumably know many nearby money speculators. Influence their system by inquiring them to acquaint you with their best customers and let them know that you will utilize them if any land bargains are made in light of the relationship!

Your Own Seminars

This one is for those of us who are all the more cordial and like to help other people with our ability. Be that as it may, in case you will be giving starting land venture workshops to individuals keen on purchasing investment properties, you will be producing your own leads and benefit from your assistance. Consider a basic sharing time kind of introduction in a lodging gathering room, with a slide show of the advantages and better yield on speculation from investment properties. A scratchpad PC and projector the inn gives are all you need, and you do a PowerPoint introduction and simply tell it as is it.

Who visits? You would advertise the FREE "Higher ROI from Rental Home Investment" class at retirement homes, with speculation counsels, in arranged advertisements, on your site, and anyplace else where a destined to-be resigned or resigned individual might be uncovered. You're demonstrating that they can do much better than the 3% returns on bank accounts and certificates of the store.

Do A Little Bit of Everything

Each technique in this section attempts to include money financial specialist purchasers in your rundown. As you produce these leads, ensure you set aside the effort to find the right pace money purchaser's purchasing criteria; furthermore, you feel are excessively genuine purchasers, I propose taking them to lunch or espresso. The more you find a workable pace, the higher your odds of selling them an arrangement!

Finding Sellers and Properties

Since we have a decent comprehension of discovering money purchasers, we talk about discovering propelled dealers. Just by the nature of our objectives as a distributor, we realize that we should be ready to purchase at a profound enough rebate to offer to our financial specialist clients, so the two gatherings can make a benefit. Along these lines, we need a critical rebate from retail, so we are looking for either bothered vendors, or upset properties. A bothered vendor is anybody encountering extreme monetary or enthusiastic torment right now, and getting money into their pocket is the answer for their concern. An upset property is any property that requires general repairs; in different words, "appalling houses." The following are only a portion of the reasons a merchant might need to sell fast for money:

- Foreclosure or default notice
- Behind in contract installments pre-notice
- Divorce
- Lost their employment or compensation cuts
- Delinquent property charges
- Death in the family
- Medical bills

- Property is in probate/acquired an undesirable house
- Home needs broad fixes
- Upside down in their home loan
- Some startling cutoff time for selling
- Tired of being a proprietor
- Legal difficulties
- Title or deed issues
- Fire/water harm

So right now, you may be asking yourself, "For what reason doesn't the vender simply list their property with a realtor"? Well, the appropriate response is simple...selling customarily requires significant investment also, sell-ing to an "all money" purchaser is quick and simple. In numerous States, the normal time it takes to sell a house by means of the MLS is 60-100+ days. Additionally, when selling customarily, the vender must locate a realtor, pay commissions, hold open houses, pay for the property to be kept up while the land operator is advertising it, pay shutting costs, and significantly after all of that, the purchaser will typically get an examination and utilize the required fixes to bring down the cost. Numerous merchants esteem speed and effortlessness over selling traditionally...and that is the reason wholesalers are near. We make a "win/win" incentive to our merchants. We get a decent arrangement, and they get quick money in their pocket, without all the run of the mill bothers of selling generally.

In the remainder of this part, we will examine various promoting procedures and strategies for finding inspired vendors that are working for wholesalers around the nation. A few or every one of them may work for you, yet you'll have to adjust and assess them in the setting of your nearby market region and the financial specialist serious condition. Recollect your incentive as a distributor is explaining property holders' monetary circumstances and giving speculators excellent arrangements. Toward the day's end, two abilities contribute legitimately to your primary concern:

- • Your capacity to find properties you can get at profound limits to current market esteem.
- • Your arrangement aptitudes on the purchasing and selling sides of the procedure.

Free Methods For Finding Sellers

We should begin with a portion of my top pick free strategies for finding inspired vendors. These will incorporate driving for dollars, setting promotions on online grouped destinations, in-person organizing, online social organizing, making offers on MLS properties, your site/ blog (SEO), and co-wholesaling other wholesalers' stock.

Driving For Dollars

For whatever length of time that there have been autos, there have been land financial specialists driving around searching for potential arrangements. The way to effectively "driving for dollars" is understanding what to search for as you drive around. Barricaded windows, congested finishing, mail/telephone directories/entryway holders accumulated on the front entryway, dispossession sees posted on the carport or front of the property, fire harm, accumulated rubbish on the property, or anything that may demonstrate that the property is surrendered or in trouble. When you discover a property that might be an up-and-comer, snap a fast photograph of the front of the property and record the address. On the off chance that you are a cordial individual and feel good, escape your vehicle and go thump on the entryway to check whether anybody is home. On the off chance that they are, at that point let them realize that you are a neighborhood financial specialist hoping to purchase a house in the area for money; furthermore, you were out conversing with every one of the neighbors to check whether they realized anybody keen on selling. On the off chance that it is empty, at that point, go thump on the neighbors' entryway and check whether you can get any data about the subject property, for example, who claimed it, to what extent has it been empty, do they have the proprietor's contact data and so on. When you return to your home or office, look into the location of the property in the district charge records. There is a site that you ought to have the option to use to discover your State's expense assessor's site, and it is called www.NETRonline.com. Snap on "Open Records Online" at that point, click on your State to pick your County. It should give all of you the data for any open workplaces, including your nearby duty assessor's site, what's more, telephone number. The objective is to look into who the "proprietor of record" is in the assessment record database and find what their "assessable postage information" is. This is the location where the proprietor of the property gets their mail. Recall this might be unique in relation to the physical property address, which is the location that you recorded when driving for dollars. Presently you have their location and name for doing a speedy pursuit on www.WhitePages.com to check whether you can uncover their telephone number. Likewise, you can send them a letter (sent to their assessable mailing advertisement dress) disclosing you need to pay money for their relinquished property!

8
MAKING TRAVEL PLANS

Regardless of whether you're going for business or delight, each outing needs a bit of arranging. Things like flights and inns must be reserved ahead of time to ensure you get the agenda you need. Travel arranging doesn't need to be distressing, however. As long as you permit yourself a lot of time to glance around, look at costs, and ensure you have all you need before you leave, you can design an exceptional travel understanding.

1) 1 Start arranging 3-6 months ahead of time. The further away you need to go, the sooner you should begin arranging. Universal outings can take a very long time to design appropriately. Moreover, trips during high seasons, for example, summer or over the memorable seasons, should be reserved farther than trips during low seasons. When in doubt, allow yourself a half year to design a global

outing, 3 months to design a local get-away, and at any rate for a month and a half for an excursion like a long end of the week. Some significant goals, for example, resorts, may require a store well ahead of time. When you choose a goal, get in touch with them to make sense of on the off chance that they need a store, and how far ahead of time, you have to pay it.

2) On the off chance that you are arranging a very late outing, be careful that you should be adaptable in where you go and precisely what your get-away will resemble. You can unquestionably design an effective a minute ago get-away; however, it frequently takes all the more moving.

3) Set a movement spending plan. Before you do anything, you have to know how much cash you will have at your removal. It's anything but difficult to overspend when you're voyaging on the off chance that you don't prepare, so start your arranging by separating the amount you need to spend on transportation, nourishment, lodging, touring, nightlife, and any different exercises you would like to remember for your trip. Your spending breakdown will fluctuate, essentially relying upon your excursion. In case you're traveling to another country, for model, a great deal of your financial limit might be devoted to transportation. In case you're arranging a nourishment visit, you may be spending a great deal on dinners yet generally little on attractions. On the off chance that you need or need to go to a particular goal, the going rates in that area will factor into setting up your spending limit. You might have the

option to discover lodging in Des Moines for $60/night, yet you won't get that equivalent arrangement in New York. Make sure to get ready for easily overlooked details like cabs or ride shares around town, the expense of boarding your pets, remote exchange charges, stuff expenses, and various deals charge rates in various districts. It's savvy to put aside about 10% of your general get-away reserve as a rainy day accounts for unpredictable conditions. Overlooking your sunscreen at home, taking a taxi since you missed the last transport, and requesting an additional beverage at supper all include. Have a crisis Mastercard if you need it, yet attempt to abstain from depending on Mastercards to control the potential for overspending.

4) Choose a goal that accommodates your accessible assets. Accessible assets incorporate not just your travel spending plan yet additionally things like what number of excursion days you have or how close you should be to a customer's office. It's enticing to go well beyond when arranging your fantasy trip; however, you'll have the most achievement if you pick a goal where you have the opportunity and cash for the sake of entertainment once you get there.

5) If, for instance, you need to take a global excursion to Paris, yet you just have two get-away days, Paris presumably isn't the correct goal as of now. You can generally decide to hold up until you have more excursion set aside or pick a goal that doesn't require enormous time responsibility for both travel and the travel industry.

6) In like manner, in the event that you are meeting a customer with workplaces downtown, don't remain in a faraway suburb to keep away from the city commotion. It can regularly require some investment to drive in the first part of the day - and that is time you could be utilized to get ready for your gathering.

7) Pick an excursion goal that you will appreciate. In case you're going for joy, search for a goal that will be pleasant for everybody going. Consider your inclinations and the interests of the individuals voyaging with you, and consider goals that work for everyone. Consider the age bunches going with you. In case you're bringing kids, search for a goal that has kid-friendly exercises. If, for instance, your youngster adores dinosaurs, check a goal's standard history historical center to check whether it has an intuitive show regarding the matter.

8) On the off chance that you and your movement colleagues like open-air exercises, check the anticipated estimate for your goal well ahead of time to ensure you can take an interest in the exercises you appreciate. Generally, climate sites and chronicles give regular climate pattern data. Consider the physical capacities of yourself and your movement friends, as well. Your maturing guardian may need to see the history in Philadelphia, for instance, however on the off chance that they have constrained versatility, the general absence of things like lifts and elevators may make it hard to visit famous goals.

9) Obtain a visa for global goals if fundamental. In case you're traveling to another country, you might be required to get an identification, visa, get specific inoculations, or give fingerprints before you withdraw. Check the site of your expected nation's department or international haven to perceive what is required for you to enter the nation. Visas may take weeks or even a long time to finish, so check right off the bat in the arranging process.

10) Various nations may have diverse passage necessities. That is why it's imperative to search for your goal nation's government office for your nation of origin. This will give you data important to you. Regardless of whether no inoculations are required for the section, it might be prudent to get them on the off chance that you are making a trip to a high-chance zone. Check with your nation's division of general wellbeing or illness control to perceive what inoculations they suggest for your planned goal.

11) Book sitters, house sitters, and pet sitters, if appropriate. If you have children or huge pets like canines, felines that aren't accompanying you when you travel, discover somebody to watch them before you book your plans. Regardless of whether you have your children remain with their grandparents for the end of the week or drop off your canine with a companion, booking early guarantees that you won't need to change your arrangements on the off chance that you can't discover the assistance you need. Whether you needn't bother with full-time care for children or pets, it might be beneficial to book a house sitter. This

individual can check your mail, water your plants, and for the most part, simply ensure that your house is all together while you're away.

12) For little pets like rodents and fish, you might have the option to request that your home sitter feed them and clean their bowl or confine them while you're gone. These pets don't need to remain with somebody full-time while you're away. One Shop around for bargains on transportation. Things like travels, flights, prepares, and even vehicle rentals can be radically extraordinary relying upon where you book them. Check the organization's site straightforwardly to search for any specials. Likewise, you should check in any event 4-5 total locales like Kayak.com, Booking.com, or Trivago to get a thought of potential value ranges.

When heading out to an alternate nation, neighborhood total booking locales may offer preferred arrangements over the ones you find in your nation of origin. Check nearby postings to check whether you can get a superior arrangement. To get the best thought of how evaluating fluctuates, think about schedules that are the equivalent. Check similar dates, what's more, goals on various destinations to see where you can truly enjoy the best arrangements.

In case you're going as a delegate of a specific organization or association, they may have an in-house travel site or travel booker that you are required to utilize. Check with your organization's managerial office to check whether that is the situation.